C★MPETITI★NS
for Talented Kids

COMPETITIONS for Talented Kids

Frances A. Karnes
& Tracy L. Riley

PRUFROCK PRESS INC.

Printed in the United States of America

Library of Congress Cataloging-in-Publication Data

Karnes, Frances A.
     Competitions for talented kids / Frances A. Karnes & Tracy L. Riley.
        p. cm.
     Includes bibliographical references and index.
     ISBN 1-59363-156-1 (alk. paper)
     1. School contests—United States. 2. Gifted children—Education—United States.
     I. Riley, Tracy L., 1966- II. Title.
     LB3068.K37 2005
     371.95'6--dc22
                                                                              2005018376

At the time of this book's publication, all facts and figures cited are the most current available. All telephone numbers, addresses, and Web site URLs are accurate and active. All publications, organizations, Web sites, and other resources exist as described in the book, and all have been verified. The authors and Prufrock Press, Inc., make no warranty or guarantee concerning the information and materials given out by organizations or content found at Web sites, and we are not responsible for any changes that occur after this book's publication. If you find an error, please contact Prufrock Press, Inc. We strongly recommend to parents, teachers, and other adults that you monitor children's use of the Internet.

Prufrock Press Inc.
P.O. Box 8813
Waco, Texas 76714-8813
(800) 998-2208
Fax (800) 240-0333
http://www.prufrock.com

For

Mary Ryan, Mo and Emma Karnes, Duncan and Shelby Riley,
Hannah and Joe Lock, and to all other children and youth who celebrate
their talents through competition.

May each of you use every opportunity available
to become the best possible you!

Table of Contents

Language Arts, Continued

Leadership

Mathematics

Performing Arts

Philosophy

Science

Visual Arts, Continued

Introduction

Competitions: What You Should Know

Have you ever created a great invention, worked on a science experiment, written an intriguing mystery, or led a service project for your community? Through competitions, you can use your skills and win in many ways. Entering competitions can be a fun and exciting part of your life.

Competition has become the backbone of our society. Adults engage in informal and formal competition nearly every day. Yet, only in the last two to three decades have competitions at the national level been available to youth. When young people participate in competitions, they are preparing to be productive adults.

There are a variety of national and international competitions identified in this book. There likely will be several in which you'll want to participate. You will discover great things about competitions. By participating, you will learn more about yourself and your special talents and abilities. Academic talents, such as language arts, science, mathematics, and social studies, as well as those in the fine and performing arts (e.g., drawing, painting, theater, and photography), can be further developed. Leadership and service learning in your school and community offer special opportunities to get involved. Most competitions in this book are open to any student, but a few require membership in an organization. Whatever your interests, this book offers a variety of competitions in which to participate.

Who Will Benefit From This Book

This book is written for elementary and secondary students. However, there are others who will also benefit from using it. Teachers will want to know the wide variety of competitions available and how to prepare their students to compete. Parents will find the number and variety of competitions of interest and will find the specifics provided helpful in assisting their children in making appropriate choices for competing. Guidance counselors and school librarians will be able to use the information to help students find appropriate outlets for their talents, as will youth group directors wanting to involve students in a wide variety of positive endeavors. Share this book with teachers, parents, or other adults who can help you and your friends become involved in competitions.

How Competitions Were Selected for This Book

Those competitions for elementary and secondary students focusing on academics, creativity, fine and performing arts, leadership, and service learning were selected for inclusion in this book. Although there are many ways to compete within your community and state, we thought having information on national competitions would help you to know about alternate ways in which to participate. It was important that most of those listed have no entrance fee, although some do require one. Much time and effort were given to locating the listed competitions. Competition sponsors also had the opportunity to submit information about their event. A few competitions chose not to be included or were uncertain of their funding for the future. If you know of competitions not listed here, please let us know for the next edition.

How to Use This Book

This book is divided into three sections. Part I includes more than 140 competitions ranging from mythology to visual arts. The competitions are listed in alphabetical order. Part II is a Competitions Journal, which provides reproducible pages for you to record your ideas about competitions. You will have an opportunity to set goals for competition, reflect upon your feelings, and investigate new areas of interest. Part III is a resource list of books that will help you as you prepare for competitions. There are books that offer everything from how to give a speech, to how to sharpen your skills as a photographer.

Thanks! Thanks! Thanks!

We would like to give special thanks to the individuals and groups who have been helpful in taking an idea and turning it into a book. We owe an enormous debt of gratitude to those adults who have conducted competitions and contributed information.

We would like to acknowledge The University of Southern Mississippi and Massey University for the support they have given us during the writing of this book.

We applaud Jennifer Jolly, our editor, for her ideas and insights. To Joel McIntosh, our publisher, we are very grateful for his interest in our ideas and for his positive personality and futuristic thinking.

Our families are constantly helpful and supportive of our professional endeavors. Our husbands, Ray and Andy, along with our families, continue to offer emotional and psychological support.

Benefits From Entering Competitions

There are many positive benefits from entering competitions. Here are a few:
- Competitions provide opportunities for growth and development of specific skills, including:
  - creative problem solving;

- critical thinking;
- leadership;
- group dynamics; and
- communication.
- Competitions build self-confidence, especially as you have the chance to feel a sense of satisfaction from accomplishments.
- Competitions serve as vehicles for self-directed learning, which makes you more responsible in planning and carrying out your goals.
- Some competitions offer opportunities for cooperative-learning experiences when you work with teams or groups of students.
- Competitions serve as outlets for displaying a variety of great products, including experiments, paintings, essays, films, inventions, photographs, songs, posters, or even sculptures.
- Competitions challenge you.
- Competitions improve your personal skills, including:
  - time management;
  - punctuality;
  - following directions;
  - meeting and greeting new and different people; and
  - responsibility and planning.
- Competitions are a constructive use of your time.
- Competitions give you a chance to experiment with some new and different "tools" for expressing yourself and your ideas.
- Competitions enhance your interests, giving you an opportunity to build on your current interests and attain new ones.
- Competitions give you a chance to meet many new people. Not only will you make new friends as you meet other students your age, you will meet many adult mentors who work in a variety of fields. Competitions serve as great networking tools.
- Competitions are a way of being recognized for your strengths, abilities, and interests.
- Competitions also offer tangible awards such as scholarships, cash prizes, trophies, ribbons, certificates, travel, or other fun prizes.

Selecting a Competition

As you go through this book and think about competitions that interest you, you'll have to make some decisions. Deciding which competitions best suit you is probably the most important one. Use the following steps to help you select a competition that will enhance your strengths and abilities.
- Assess your talent area. Ask yourself, "What talents do I have?" List the areas in which you do very well. Some ideas might be: math, science, history, reading, drawing, creative writing, singing, playing the piano, photography, or leadership.

- List your interests.
- List things you would like to learn more about or areas you would like to improve.
- Combine these lists. Rank order the items and select the top five areas.
- Select several competitions that may help you improve and build on your strengths and interests.
- Read the description for each competition. Ask yourself the following questions:
  - Can I do what is expected?
  - Is this competition in my area of ability and/or interest?
  - Do I have the time to participate?
  - Do I have the resources for participation?
  - Will I need a sponsor? If so, can I get one? How can I get one?
  - If a team is needed, are there other students interested?
  - Is my idea practical and original?
- Discuss your ideas with a teacher, your parents, and friends. Seek their advice. They may give you some really good ideas, but remember, they may not tell you what you want to hear. Take the suggestions that are good for you and keep working toward your goal.
- Talk to other students who have participated in the competition you selected (or one similar to it). Ask them about their experiences.
- Brainstorm and write down the positive and negative aspects of entering the competition.
- Be sure to check your calendar.
- Select a competition based upon this assessment and have a fantastic time preparing for and participating in it.
- Evaluate yourself and the competition. Reflect on the experience, celebrate your efforts, and set new goals for future competitions.

Things to Keep in Mind

Competitions and competing can be a positive or negative experience, depending on why you want to be involved. Being in a contest can help you improve and achieve, not only in the area of the competition, but also in interpersonal and personal skills. You will discover a new sense of motivation, energy, and self-confidence to improve, persevere, and excel. You will be able to gauge your own abilities against those of others. As you do so, you will find yourself working harder toward reaching your goals.

In setting your competition goals, plan to become involved only in those competitions for which you have the time, abilities, and interests. Set your own priorities and stick to them. Keep yourself balanced and don't overload yourself with too many competitive events.

Overcompetitiveness can lead to some possible pitfalls. Some people may let their personal values and ethics go by the wayside and not do the right things just to win. Too much rivalry may result in hurt feelings among friends. You may put yourself under too much pressure and set yourself up for feelings of failure. Keep your sense of humor, and if you are feeling stressed out, always remember that good health and exercise have been shown to help relieve stress and anxiety.

One major stress factor in becoming involved in competitions is the possibility of winning or losing. What if you don't win? Of course, you will be disappointed and unhappy. It is only natural to feel that way. But, remember, competitions are learning experiences in themselves. Consider all the knowledge you'll obtain, the friends you'll make, and the opportunities you'll experience.

You can also think about what you did and how you can improve. It often helps to record your ideas in a Competitions Journal. After the competition, ask yourself the following questions:

- What did I learn?
- What did I do right?
- What could I have done better?
- What do I need to do in order to do better in the future?

After examining your answers to these questions, you will want to get involved in competitions again. Feel good about yourself. Strive for improving yourself and becoming the best possible. Most importantly, remember to have fun doing it.

★ ★

Members Only

There are several organizations, associations, and clubs that have competitions for members only. Usually, a membership fee and active group participation are required. You may already belong to one or more of these through your school or community involvement. If you would like more information, there are a couple of ways to get it. Look in your local telephone directory to see if there is a local group, or ask your school counselor or principal if your school already has one. Another way to find what you need to know is to write directly to the organization or visit its Web site. Listed below is a sampling of organizations, clubs, and associations that require membership.

American Morgan Horse Association
122 Bostwick Road
Shelburne, VT 05482-4417
http://www.morganhorse.com

Boys and Girls Clubs of America
1230 W. Peachtree St., NW
Atlanta, GA 30309
http://www.bgca.org

Boy Scouts of America
1325 Walnut Hill Lane
Irving, TX 75015-2079
http://www.scouting.org

Business Professionals of America
5454 Cleveland Ave.
Columbus, OH 43231-4021
http://www.bpa.org

Future Business Leaders of America
1912 Association Dr.
Reston, VA 20191-1591
http://www.fbla-pbl.org

Girls Inc.
120 Wall St.
New York, NY 10005-3902
http://www.girlsinc.org/ic

Girl Scouts of the United States
of America
420 Fifth Ave.
New York, NY 10018-2798
http://www.girlscouts.org

Health Occupations Students
of America
6021 Morris Rd., Ste. 111
Flower Mound, TX 75028
http://www.hosa.org

Key Club International
3636 Woodview Trace
Indianapolis, IN 46268
http://www.keyclub.org/keyclub

National Beta Club
151 Beta Club Way
Spartanburg, SC 29306-3012
http://www.betaclub.org

National DECA Club
1908 Association Dr.
Reston, VA 20191
http://www.deca.org

National Forensic League
P.O. Box 38, 125 Watson St.
Ripon, WI 54971
http://www.nflonline.org

National Future Farmers of America
P.O. Box 68960, 6060 FFA Dr.
Indianapolis, IN 46268-0960
http://www.ffa.org

National Junior Classical League
422 Wells Mill Dr.
Miami University
Oxford, OH 45056
http://www.njcl.org/activities

National Junior Horticultural
Association
15 R. R. Ave.
Homer City, PA 15748
http://www.njha.org

National Management Association
2210 Arbor Blvd.
Dayton, OH 45439
http://www.nma1.org

National Scholastic Press Association
2221 University Ave. SE, Ste. 121
Minneapolis, MN 55414
http://www.studentpress.org/nspa

Quill and Scroll Society
School of Journalism
The University of Iowa
Iowa City, IA 52242
http://www.uiowa.edu/~quill-sc

Technology Student Association
1914 Association Dr.
Reston, VA 20191-1540
http://www.tsawww.org

United States Chess Federation
3054 U.S. Route 9W
New Windsor, NY 12553
http://www.uschess.org

United States Department of
Agriculture Cooperative State Research,
Education, and Extension Service
1400 Independence Avenue SW,
Stop 2201
Washington, DC 20250-2201
http://www.csrees.usda.gov

★ PART I ★
List of Competitions

Competition★	**AAA National School Traffic Safety Poster Program**
Sponsor★	American Automobile Association 1000 AAA Dr. Heathrow, FL 32746-5063
Web Address★	http://www.aaasouth.com/ts_contest.asp
Area★	Visual arts
Competition Origin★	1945
Purpose★	To teach and promote traffic safety.
Description★	Students create and execute a chosen traffic safety slogan in the form of a poster. The poster must be 15" x 20", 14" x 22", or 12" x 18" with a 3" margin across the bottom of the poster for the entry blank and administrative purposes. Guidelines are available from the local main AAA club office or by visiting the Web site.
Eligibility★	Students in grades K–12. There are four grade divisions: Primary (K–2); Elementary (3–5); Junior High (6–8); and Senior High (9–12).
Important Dates★	Posters are due in February. See guidelines for specific dates.
How to Enter★	Mail the finished poster to either the local office of AAA or to AAA National Headquarters as noted in the brochure guidelines.
Judging Criteria★	Relationship of the poster design to traffic safety practices, originality of the poster, artwork, and execution.
Judges★	A panel of prominent individuals in the fields of education, art, and traffic safety.
Winner Notification★	Winners will be notified by local AAA Clubs.
Awards★	Winners share more than $18,000 in Visa Gift Checks.
Advice★	Have a focal point, and keep it simple. Use contrasting colors. Viewers must be able to read your ideas quickly.

Competition★	**AATSP (American Association of Teachers of Spanish and Portuguese) FLES (Foreign Language Elementary School) Elementary/Middle School Poster Contest**
Sponsor★	The American Association of Teachers of Spanish and Portuguese 423 Exton Commons Exton, PA 19341-2451
Web Address★	https://www.aatsp.org
Areas★	Foreign language and visual arts
Competition Origin★	Mid-1980s
Purpose★	For students of Spanish or Portuguese to express their ideas and understandings of language and culture through drawing.
Description★	Entries must be 12" x 18" and may be drawn in pencil, crayon, pen, ink, or markers. They may include captions in Spanish, Portuguese, or English. Visit the Web site for guidelines and an application.
Eligibility★	Students in grades K–8. There are three grade divisions: K–3; 4–5; and 6–8.
Important Dates★	Entries are due in April. See guidelines for specific dates.
How to Enter★	Students must be sponsored by a teacher who is a member of AATSP. Submissions need to be made following the application guidelines on the Web site.
Judging Criteria★	Applicability to the annual theme, uniqueness, and creativity.
Judges★	Members of AATSP FLES Poster Contest Committee.
Winner Notification★	Winners are notified by the end of May.
Awards★	Prizes will be awarded for the first-, second-, and third-place winners in each of the grade categories. Each entry will also receive a poster contest certificate suitable for framing.

Competition★ Academic Games Leagues of America National Tournament

Sponsor★ Academic Games Leagues of America, Inc.
P.O. Box 17563
West Palm Beach, FL 33406

Web Address★ http://academicgames.org/national.htm

Areas★ Language arts, mathematics, and social studies

Competition Origin★ 1966

Purpose★ To challenge capable students in mathematics, social studies, and language arts and to provide recognition for these outstanding students.

Description★ Teams are composed of five players. Each player plays in a three-person match for 30 minutes. The national tournament takes place over 4 days at a different site each year. Local league "seasons" vary from 1-day tournaments to eight rounds over 8 weeks. Visit the Web site for information regarding dates, costs, and deadlines, as well as registration forms.

Eligibility★ Students in grades 4–12. There are four grade divisions: Elementary (4–6); Middle (7–8); Junior (9–10); and Senior (11–12).

Important Dates★ Registration deadlines begin in January. The national tournament is held in April each year. See guidelines for specific dates.

How to Enter★ Contact a local league or visit the Web site.

Judging Criteria★ In accordance with each game's rules.

Judges★ Judging is conducted by local teachers and officials. Judging assistance is provided for new programs.

Winner Notification★ Winners are notified at the site of each tournament.

Awards★ Local league awards are arranged from local sponsors. National tournament awards and scholarships are presented on site and vary yearly.

Advice★ These competitions foster the same type of team camaraderie as most sports teams. Students are challenged to apply their knowledge and skills. Information about each game's rules and purposes are located on the Web site.

Competition★	Achievement Awards in Writing
Sponsor★	National Council of Teachers of English 1111 W. Kenyon Road Urbana, IL 61801-1096
Web Address★	http://www.ncte.org
Area★	Language arts
Competition Origin★	1957
Purpose★	To encourage high school juniors in their writing and to recognize publicly some of the best student writers in the nation.
Description★	Students submit two pieces of original writing. The first is an impromptu essay, and the second is a best writing sample, which may consist of prose and/or verse. Contact the sponsor for a brochure or visit the Web site.
Eligibility★	Students in grade 11.
Important Dates★	Deadline for nominations by teachers is late January. Topics are mailed in March, and entries are sent to state coordinators in April. State coordinators mail results to NCTE in August. See guidelines for specific dates.
How to Enter★	Students must be nominated by their English teachers.
Judging Criteria★	Depth of thought in quality and presentation of ideas; student ownership of ideas; clarity of subject and audience; and command of vocabulary and sentence structure.
Judges★	Each state coordinator selects a team of judges, consisting of high school and college English teachers.
Winner Notification★	Winners are notified in October.
Awards★	Each winner receives a certificate, booklet, letter, and scholastic form. Cards stating that they are winners are also sent and can be attached to college applications in order to assist with financial needs or college entry.
Advice★	Tenth graders with outstanding writing skills should contact the 11th-grade English teacher now.

Competition★	**ACL/NJCL National Greek Examination**
Sponsor★	ACL/NJCL National Greek Examination The American Classical League Miami University Oxford, OH 45056
Web Address★	http://nle.aclclassics.org
Area★	Foreign language
Competition Origin★	1980
Purpose★	To provide first-, second-, and third-year high school and college students of Attic or Homeric Greek with an examination by which they can measure their achievement against that of students in other schools.
Description★	The usual sequence of exams is Introduction to Greek, Beginning Attic, Intermediate Attic, Attic Prose, and Attic Tragedy. Students take the exam that most closely matches their experience. Each examination lasts 50 minutes and contains 40 questions with multiple-choice answers. Guidelines and syllabi may be obtained by writing to the sponsor.
Eligibility★	Students in grades 9–12 and college.
Important Dates★	The examination date is in early March. See guidelines for specific dates.
How to Enter★	Contact your school guidance counselor, principal, or teacher.
Judging Criteria★	Accuracy of answers.
Judges★	The exams are graded by computer.
Winner Notification★	Winners are notified upon completion of grading, typically at the end of April.
Awards★	Winners receive purple, blue, red, or green ribbons and hand-lettered certificates, which are mailed to the Greek teacher at each participating school the last 2 weeks of April. A typed list with the names of all the winners, their ranks, and schools is mailed at the same time. Winners are also announced on the Web site. Purple ribbon winners may apply for a $1,000 scholarship.

Advice★

A packet of previous exams can be obtained from the sponsor for a small fee. Applications for this contest are only accepted from teachers, and entrants pay a fee for each exam.

Competition★	**Adlyn M. Keffer National Story League Short Story Writing Contest**
Sponsor★	Adlyn M. Keffer National Story League 10 Woodside Dr., Lumberton Leas Lumberton, NJ 08048
Web Address★	http://www.concentric.net/~Lkbenoun/ national_story_league.htm
Area★	Language arts
Competition Origin★	1952
Purpose★	To encourage short-story writing.
Description★	Students submit an original short story of 2,000 words or less. Contact the National Story League for guidelines.
Eligibility★	Students in grades 4–12. There are two grade divisions: 4–8 and 9–12.
Important Dates★	The contest begins in January and ends at the end of March. See guidelines for specific dates.
How to Enter★	Three copies of an original story must be submitted—typed on white 8½" x 11" paper, double-spaced, and on one side of the page only. Story must not exceed 2,000 words. Numbers of words in the story should be placed in upper right-hand corner of the title page. Only one entry will be accepted from each contestant. No identifying marks or names should appear on the manuscript or title page. On a separate page put the title of the story, name and address of the author, and whether the author is an adult or a minor. On this page also indicate membership in a story league or youth group, including the name of the school and sponsor's name if applicable.
Judging Criteria★	Entries are judged on originality, tellability, title, beginning, plot, characters, language, grammar, ending, and proper submission.
Judges★	There are three judges, one appointed by each district president with the approval of the NSL president. Judges' names will be published in *Story Art* magazine when winners are announced.

★ ★

Winner Notification★

Winners are notified by sponsor at the beginning of May.

Awards★

Three prizes of $40, $30, and $20 will be awarded. There may be up to three honorable mentions.

Advice★

All stories submitted must be original and will become the property of the National Story League. No manuscripts will be returned. Author retains all rights except first publication rights of the stories published in *Story Art* magazine. All rights revert to the author if the story is not published in *Story Art* or 1 year from the time stories are received by *Story Art*. Evaluation sheets are available in May from the chairman for the costs of copying and postage.

Competition★	**All-USA High School Academic Team Competition**
Sponsor★	*USA Today* 7950 Jones Branch Dr. McLean, VA, 22108-9995
Web Address★	http://www.usatoday.com/news/education/ 2002-11-04-allstars_x.htm
Areas★	Academic recognition, leadership, and visual arts
Competition Origin★	1986
Purpose★	To recognize academic excellence by honoring outstanding high school students.
Description★	This program acknowledges not only academic abilities, but also other talents such as the arts and leadership. Guidelines may be obtained on the Web site or by writing to the sponsor.
Eligibility★	Students graduating from grade 12.
Important Dates★	High school nomination forms are available in December. Forms are due in late February. See guidelines for specific dates.
How to Enter★	Nomination forms are mailed to all high school principals and guidance directors in the U.S. and American schools overseas, or they can be requested from the sponsor.
Judging Criteria★	Judges base their decisions on students' outstanding original academic, artistic, and leadership endeavors.
Judges★	High school teachers and principals selected by the sponsor.
Winner Notification★	Winners are notified in May.
Awards★	Twenty students are named to the first team, and each receives a cash award of $2,500, a trophy, and recognition in *USA Today*. Up to 40 runners-up are named to the second and third teams. They are named in the paper and receive certificates of achievement.

Competition★	**American Association of Teachers of French (AATF) National French Contest**
Sponsor★	American Association of Teachers of French (AATF) Mailcode 4510 Southern Illinois University Carbondale, IL 62901-4510
Web Address★	http://www.frenchteachers.org/concours
Area★	Foreign language
Competition Origin★	1993
Purpose★	To motivate students in teaching and learning French.
Description★	Students take a 60-minute exam constructed by the American Association of Teachers of French. Guidelines may be obtained on the Web site or by writing to the sponsor.
Eligibility★	Students of French in grades 1–12.
Important Dates★	Dates vary in February and March according to each grade level. See guidelines for specific dates.
How to Enter★	French teachers must enter students. The teachers will have to contact their local contest administrator, who can be found through the Web site or by contacting the sponsor.
Judging Criteria★	Accuracy of answers.
Judges★	AATF computer scoring.
Winner Notification★	Winners are notified in a "timely fashion."
Awards★	There are two categories of awards: chapter and national. Chapters offer prizes to those students who are among the top scorers at the chapter level for each level and division. National prizes are subsidized out of the fees paid by each entrant. Prizes awarded by Le Grand Concours include French videos, medals, and books. In addition, various French firms donate prizes, which are distributed to national winners.
Advice★	It is a good idea for teachers to enter all of their students in the contest, not just potential winners.

Competition★	**American Association of Teachers of German (AATG) National German Testing Program for High School Students**
Sponsor★	American Association of Teachers of German, Inc. 112 Haddontowne Court #104 Cherry Hill, NJ 08034-3668
Web Address★	http://www.aatg.org/programs/hsstudentprogs/ testing_program/testing_info.html
Area★	Foreign language
Competition Origin★	1970
Purpose★	To increase student interest in proficiency in German.
Description★	Students are administered the AATG test in their schools. Write for guidelines in September or visit the Web site year-round.
Eligibility★	Students who are enrolled in second-, third-, or fourth-year German classes. Those scoring at or above the 90th percentile are eligible to apply for a study trip to Germany (if applicable).
Important Dates★	Teachers may order the tests from October to December. Testing takes place in December and January. See guidelines for specific dates.
How to Enter★	Contact the German teacher in the local high school.
Judging Criteria★	Accuracy of answers.
Judges★	Testing committee.
Winner Notification★	Winners are notified in March.
Awards★	Many chapters honor students at awards ceremonies, luncheons, and dinners with prizes, including certificates for placing at the 70th percentile and above, books, special medals, T-shirts, savings bonds, and cash. In the past, study trips have been awarded to students selected by a national committee.
Advice★	Teachers should enroll all students of German in the competition.

Competition★	**American Computer Science League (ACSL) Competitions**
Sponsor★	American Computer Science League Box 521 West Warwick, RI 02893
Web Address★	http://www.acsl.org
Area★	Technology
Competition Origin★	1979
Purpose★	To provide a unique and exciting educational opportunity for computer enthusiasts. Contest problems motivate students to study computer topics not covered in their school's curricula and to pursue classroom topics in-depth.
Description★	Contests are held at each participating school, and an unlimited number of students may compete. A school's score is the sum of the scores of its three or five highest scoring students. In each competition, students are given short theoretical and applied questions, and then a practical problem to solve within the following 3 days, testing it on data using their school's computer facilities. After the contest is administered by the faculty advisor, each school's results are returned to ACSL for tabulation. At the end of the year, an Invitational Team All-Star Contest is held at a common site. The Classroom Division consists of only pencil-and-paper questions; there are no programming problems. This division is open to all students from all grades not competing in any other division. Guidelines may be obtained on the Web site or by writing to the sponsor.
Eligibility★	Students in grades 6–12. There are four divisions: Classroom Division (all grades); Junior Division (junior high and middle school students with no previous experience); Intermediate Division (non-experienced high school students and advanced junior high students); and Senior Division (experienced high school students).
Important Dates★	Schools begin registering in July. Contests are administered in December, February, March, and April. See guidelines for specific dates.

Judging Criteria★ Accuracy of answers.

Judges★ Local schools score results.

Winner Notification★ The All-Star Team is announced in May.

Awards★ Prizes are awarded on a grade-by-grade basis. At the All-Star Contest, the top two schools in each division are awarded a CD/DVD Rewrite Drive. The top three schools, as well as each team member, also receive trophies. Top-scoring students at the All-Star Contest are awarded books donated by publishers. All students are given request forms to receive software from Microsoft. Trophies are awarded to the top teams and the top individuals in each regional area of each division. Finally, each team receives an award to present to an outstanding student at the advisor's discretion.

Advice★ Awards may vary due to changes in sponsorship and resources each year. There are sample problems and solutions on the Web site.

Competition★	**American High School Theatre Festival**
Sponsor★	American High School Theatre Festival 590 Peter Jefferson Pl., Ste. 300 Charlottesville, VA 22901
Web Address★	http://www.ahstf.com
Area★	Performing arts
Competition Origin★	1994
Purpose★	To complement high school drama programs and allow the nation's drama students to showcase their skills within an international forum.
Description★	Selected schools attend the Edinburgh Fringe Festival, the world's largest performing arts festival. Guidelines may be obtained on the Web site or by writing to the sponsor.
Eligibility★	High school theatre groups are eligible for nomination. Nominations may only be submitted by college or university professors; state, regional, or national theatre organization or association members; or past alumni (winning teachers) of AHSTF.
Important Dates★	Nominations must be received by mid-November. Applications are mailed to nominees in December and must be completed by early February. See guidelines for specific dates.
How to Enter★	Nominations may be submitted online at the Web site.
Judging Criteria★	Top high school programs are selected based upon their most recent bodies of work, awards, community involvement, philosophies, and recommendations.
Judges★	Each nominated school receives an application, and all completed applications are reviewed by the AHSTF Board of Advisors. The panel of college theatre professionals comes from all corners of the country.
Winner Notification★	Selected schools are notified by August.
Awards★	Round-trip airfare to London; guided tour of London; two nights' London accommodation; West End theatre performance; private chartered train from London to Edinburgh; tube/bus half-day

guided sightseeing in Edinburgh and full-day countryside trip on chartered motor coaches; four performance slots at AHSTF's international venue; two meals daily; 10 nights accommodations in Edinburgh; AHSTF welcome reception and post-program awards ceremony; and admission to Military Tattoo on the grounds of the Edinburgh Castle.

Advice★   Self-nominations are not accepted.

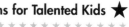

Competition★	**American History Essay Contest**
Sponsor★	National Society Daughters of the American Revolution 1776 D St. N.W. Washington, DC 20006-5303
Web Address★	http://www.dar.org/natsociety
Areas★	Social studies and language arts
Competition Origin★	1966
Purpose★	To encourage and reward good citizenship and historical understandings.
Description★	A selected essay topic for use during the academic year is announced, and contest instructions are sent to the schools by participating chapters on a yearly basis. Information can be obtained through the DAR state chairperson in your state.
Eligibility★	Students in grades 5–8.
Important Dates★	Contact your local chapter or visit the Web site for deadlines.
How to Enter★	Contact the DAR chapter of the state in which the student resides.
Judging Criteria★	Essays are judged for historical accuracy, adherence to topic, organization of materials, interest, originality, spelling, grammar, punctuation, and neatness.
Judges★	State-level judging is determined by each chapter; judging at the national level is supervised by the DAR National Society. The winning essay from each of the four grades on the regional level will be judged on the national level.
Winner Notification★	Winners are notified after the national-level judging is complete.
Awards★	Each student participant receives a certificate of participation by the chapter, and the chapter winners receive bronze medals and certificates. State winners receive certificates and silver medals. National winners receive special certificates, medals, and a monetary award.

Competition★	**American Mathematics Competitions (AMC)**
Sponsor★	The American Mathematics Competitions Prof. Steven Dunbar University of Nebraska–Lincoln Lincoln, NE 68588-0658
Web Address★	http://www.unl.edu/amc/whatswhat.html
Area★	Mathematics
Competition Origin★	1950
Purpose★	To provide a friendly challenge to students, as well as an opportunity to recognize mathematical talent.
Description★	National contests called the American Mathematics Contest 8 (AMC 8); the American Mathematics Contest 10 (AMC 10); the American Mathematics Contest 12 (AMC 12); the American Invitational Mathematics Examination (AIME); and the United States of America Mathematical Olympiad (USAMO) are held each year. Contests consist of multiple-choice or essay/proof tests of mathematics. Guidelines are available early in the school year.
Eligibility★	Students in grades 6–12.
Important Dates★	Dates vary with each contest, but are from March to May each year. See guidelines for specific dates.
How to Enter★	Contact the sponsor.
Judging Criteria★	Accuracy of answers.
Judges★	Tests are scored electronically.
Winner Notification★	Winners are notified upon receipt and scoring of exams.
Awards★	The top participants are recognized as Honor Roll students. The Honor Roll students are invited to take the American Invitational Mathematics Examination in March, and the top 250 students are invited to participate in the USA Mathematical Olympiad in April.

Competition★	**American Regions Mathematics League Competition**
Sponsor★	American Regions Mathematics League 4505-6 Staffordshire Dr. Wilmington, NC 28412
Web Address★	http://arml.com
Area★	Mathematics
Competition Origin★	1975
Purpose★	To make students more comfortable with their abilities and introduce them to new and exciting areas of math.
Description★	The annual competition is designed for both teams and individuals on the teams. The team round consists of short-answer questions the team members work on cooperatively. The Power Round forces the team to use various methods of mathematical analysis and proof; members must then expand and generalize from the topic. The conclusions are put together in the form of a report. The Individual Round allows participants to work independently on several questions within a mandated time frame. The Relay Round sets up "subteams" within a team: The answer to one team member's question is used by another to answer the next. Credit is given only if the final team member answers correctly. Guidelines may be obtained on the Web site or by writing to the sponsor.
Eligibility★	Students in grades 6–12 (the contest is written for high school students, but exceptional junior high students can compete).
Important Dates★	See guidelines for specific dates.
How to Enter★	Write to the sponsor for entry information or obtain an entry form online.
Judging Criteria★	Varies with each competition. Accuracy of answers is the key factor.
Judges★	American Regions Mathematics League officials and volunteers.
Winner Notification★	Winners are notified at each stage of competition.

Awards★	All participants receive a certificate for participation. Other prizes include trophies and plaques.
Advice★	Previous years' exams are available online.

Competition★	**AMVETS Americanism Program**
Sponsor★	AMVETS and AMVETS Auxiliary Program National Headquarters 4647 Forbes Blvd. Lanham, MD 20706-4380.
Web Address★	http://www.amvets.org
Areas★	Language arts, social studies, and visual arts
Competition Origin★	1950s
Purpose★	To promote Americanism through drawing and essay writing.
Description★	This patriotic program helps teach students about their American heritage, civics, and citizenship. Students design flags, posters, or write essays. Contact the sponsor for the guidelines.
Eligibility★	Students in grades K–12. There are three grade divisions: Flag Drawing (K–1); Poster Contest (2–5); and Essay Writing (6–12).
Important Dates★	Local entries are due to local AMVETS departments at least 30 days before the national deadline, where they are judged and submitted for national consideration. The national deadline is in July. See guidelines for specific dates.
How to Enter★	Application is available online and from the local sponsor.
Judging Criteria★	Entries are judged on originality, adherence to theme, and literary composition.
Judges★	Local and national judges appointed by AMVETS.
Winner Notification★	Varies with local contest dates.
Awards★	Winners receive savings bonds. All ninth-grade first-place winners receive a trip to Valley Forge for a long weekend of youth activities.

Competition★	**AMVETS National Americanism Poster Contest**
Sponsor★	AMVETS National Headquarters 1000 S. 4th St. Louisville, KY 40203
Web Address★	http://www.sar.org
Area★	Visual arts
Competition Origin★	2000s
Purpose★	To promote Americanism among youth.
Description★	All students must address the theme, which changes annually. Entries must be freehand drawings using pen, pencil, crayon, paint, or any combination of these materials. Gluing pictures or other materials to the surface of the drawing is not allowed. The student's description of the drawing must be written on the back of the poster in 50 words or less. Entries must be on 9" x 12" construction paper or poster board. Contact the sponsor for the guidelines.
Eligibility★	Students in grades 2–5.
Important Dates★	Local and state dealines vary. The national deadline is in July. See guidelines for specific dates.
How to Enter★	Contact your local sponsor.
Judging Criteria★	Posters are judged on artistic ability, adherence to the theme, and neatness.
Judges★	Local and national judges appointed by AMVETS.
Winner Notification★	Varies with local contest dates.
Awards★	First-, second-, and third-place winners receive savings bonds, ranging from $100 to $300.
Advice★	Contact your local or state chapter early in the school year for details.

Competition★	**Ann Arlys Bowler Poetry Contest**
Sponsor★	Weekly Reader Corp. 200 First Stamford Pl. P.O. Box 120023 Stamford, CT 06912-0023
Web Address★	https://www.weeklyreader.com/teachers/read/ bowlers_con.asp
Area★	Language arts
Competition Origin★	1989
Purpose★	To award fine poetic creativity and to encourage writing for middle school and high school students.
Description★	This is an annual poetry contest. The winners are published in an all-student-written issue of *Read* in April. Guidelines may be obtained on the Web site or by writing to the sponsor.
Eligibility★	Students in grades 6–12.
Important Dates★	Entries must be received by the end of January. See guidelines for specific dates.
How to Enter★	Write to the sponsor for full guidelines and entry coupon. Entry forms are also available online.
Judging Criteria★	Entries must be original, not previously published, show excellent command of English, have spark, and appeal to middle school readers.
Judges★	*Weekly Reader* editorial staff members.
Winner Notification★	Winners are notified in April.
Awards★	Six winners receive $100, an engraved medal, a certificate of excellence, and publication in *Read* magazine. Six semifinalists receive $50, a certificate of excellence, and publication on *Read*'s Web site.
Advice★	Entries should be typed, doubled-spaced, and no longer than one page, and the entry coupon must be filled out and stapled to the back.

Competition★	**Annual Math League Contests**
Sponsor★	Mathematics Leagues P.O. Box 17 Tenafly, NJ 07670-0017
Web Address★	http://www.mathleague.com/contests.htm
Area★	Mathematics
Competition Origin★	1977
Purpose★	To encourage student interest and confidence in mathematics through problem-solving activities.
Description★	Mathematic contests comprised of timed multiple-choice tests. Guidelines are posted throughout the year and may be obtained through the Web site.
Eligibility★	Students in grades 4–12.
Important Dates★	Dates will vary for each grade level. See guidelines for specific dates.
How to Enter★	You may register through the Web site. You may also print an order form from the Web site and mail it to the sponsor.
Judging Criteria★	Accuracy of answers.
Judges★	The contest is scored by machines.
Winner Notification★	Varies with competition deadlines.
Awards★	Certificates for high scorers and certificates of achievement are awarded.
Advice★	Sample tests are on the Web site.

Competition★	**Arts Recognition and Talent Search (ARTS) Program**
Sponsor★	National Foundation for Advancement in the Arts 800 Brickell Ave., P-14 Miami, FL 33131
Web Address★	http://www.artsawards.org
Areas★	Performing arts and visual arts
Competition Origin★	1981
Purpose★	To recognize young American artists of exceptional ability and provide them with the opportunity to be evaluated by panels of experts in their field, considered for scholarships offered by NFAA's Scholarship List Service subscriber, receive unrestricted cash grants, participate in ARTS Week, be nominated to the White House Commission on Presidential Scholars, and benefit from NFAA's ongoing support of its alumni through various internship and career advancement programs.
Description★	Of the more than 7,000 high-school-senior-age artists who apply, approximately 350 earn ARTS awards. Of that number, 120 will be invited, at NFAA's expense, to participate in ARTS Week, 6 full days of judged individual auditions, workshops, master classes, and seminars in Miami, FL. Up to 50 top ARTS awardees are nominated by NFAA to the White House Commission on Presidential Scholars for designation as U.S. Presidential Scholars in the Arts, the highest honor bestowed on graduating American high school seniors who excel in the arts. Ultimately, 20 are chosen for this prestigious award and honored at a White House ceremony during National Recognition Week in June. All students who participate in ARTS are eligible for more than $3 million in scholarship opportunities offered by more than 100 colleges, universities, and professional arts institutions. Guidelines may be obtained on the Web site or by writing to the sponsor.
Eligibility★	Students in grade 12. Students not enrolled in high school (whether enrolled in college, a high school graduate not enrolled in college, or an individual not

completing high school) must be 17 or 18 years old on December 1.

Important Dates★
Deadlines are in June and October. See guidelines for specific dates.

How to Enter★
Complete the ARTS registration form and send it along with appropriate fees. You will then receive a detailed packet of instructions along with a program identification number. Applicants need to read the packet information very carefully and follow directions.

Judging Criteria★
The judges, using a two-step process, review materials submitted by the applicants, selecting up to 20 award candidates in each of the eight disciplines for live adjudications in Miami. An unlimited number of $100 Honorable Mention awards are granted to selected applicants who are not invited to Miami.

Judges★
Panels of experts—one panel for each art discipline.

Winner Notification★
In December, winners are notified of their invitation to Miami for ARTS Week.

Awards★
Some students are invited to Miami for ARTS Week, a week of live adjudications consisting of auditions, master and technique classes, workshops, studio exercises, and interviews. NFAA pays round trip airfare within the U.S. and its territories, lodging, and meal expenses. Winners receive: Gold awards, $10,000; first-level awards, $3,000; second-level awards, $1,500; third-level awards, $1,000; fourth-level awards, $500; and fifth-level awards, $50.

Competition★	**Baker's Plays High School Playwriting Contest**
Sponsor★	Baker's Plays P.O. Box 699222 Quincy, MA 02269-9222
Web Address★	http://bakersplays.com/bsubmit.htm#HSCONTEST
Areas★	Language arts and performing arts
Competition Origin★	1990
Purpose★	To encourage creative writing in high school students through the creation of original plays for publication.
Description★	Students submit bound, typed manuscripts with self-addressed, stamped envelopes. Plays are judged on their originality and quality of writing appropriate for a high school audience. Guidelines are available on the sponsor's Web site.
Eligibility★	Students in grades 9–12.
Important Dates★	Submit plays at the end of January. See guidelines for specific dates.
How to Enter★	See guidelines on Web site.
Judging Criteria★	Awards are based on merit, and if no submission warrants an award, no prizes are given.
Judges★	Nominees of sponsor.
Awards★	First-place winner receives $500 and Baker's Plays publishes his or her play with a royalty-earning contract; $250 and an honorable mention for second place; and $100 and an honorable mention for third place.
Winner Notification★	Winners are notified in May.
Advice★	Content of the plays should include the "high school experience," but may be about any subject. Plays may be any length, but should be written so that they can be reasonably produced on the high school stage. The sponsor prefers plays that have been production tested. Plays that have had a staged reading, workshop reading, or full production usually undergo revisions during the rehearsal process. If your play has not yet been produced, your time and energy may be better first spent pursuing a production, rather than publication.

Competition★	**BEST Robotics**
Sponsor★	BEST Robotics, Inc., a Web-based organization. (The Web site has e-mail details for personal contact.)
Web Address★	http://www.bestinc.org
Areas★	Engineering, science, and technology
Competition Origin★	1994
Purpose★	To promote teamwork, problem solving, project management, and pride.
Description★	In a 6-week period students have to create a radio-controlled robot along with a project notebook, oral presentation, and an interview. Each student also works with teams ranging anywhere from 5–60 students. The guidelines can be obtained by contacting the local sponsor by e-mail or through the Web site.
Eligibility★	Students in grades 6–12.
Important Dates★	The regional competitions are held in mid-November. See guidelines for specific dates.
How to Enter★	Participants may register online through the Web site.
Judging Criteria★	Students are judged on creativity, the use of technology, publicity, presentation, participation, enthusiasm, sportsmanship, and robot performance.
Judges★	Engineers and other technical professionals.
Winner Notification★	Winners are notified at local and regional tournament sites.
Awards★	First-, second-, and third-place awards are given along with several other special awards such as the BEST Award, Competition Award, Founders Award for Creative Design, Most Robust, Most Elegant, Most Photogenic, T-Shirt Award, and Web Page Award.
Advice★	Anyone—colleges/universities, corporations, individuals—can start a new hub serving a minimum of eight teams. The average first-year cost for running a 24-team hub is approximately $28,000. Local hubs rely on financial support from corporations and/or colleges/universities in order to allow schools to participate at no cost.

Competition★	Biz Plan Competition
Sponsor★	Independent Means, Inc. 126 East Haley St., #A-16 Santa Barbara, CA 93101
Web Address★	http://www.independentmeans.com/imi/dollardiva/bizplan/index.php
Area★	Business
Competition Origin★	1992
Purpose★	To give young women an opportunity to increase their understanding of the concepts, tools, and responsibilities of business ownership while putting their own entrepreneurial dreams on paper.
Description★	The competition's application provides entrants with an introduction on how to prepare a business plan and challenges them to apply and modify the basic format to fit their business idea. The message is that entrepreneurs can find themselves on a path to creativity, economic security, and fun. Applications are available on the Web site or by contacting the sponsor.
Eligibility★	Females ages 13–21 as of August 15.
Important Dates★	Applications must be submitted in mid-November. See guidelines for specific dates.
How to Enter★	The application form can be downloaded from the Web site.
Judging Criteria★	The business plan can be no longer than 10 pages and must be accompanied by the Adult Consent Form found in the application. Entries are judged on the quality of the business plan produced, and no extra points are given for entrants who actually have a business or create the business described in the plan.
Judges★	Business owners with practical experience writing and implementing business plans.
Winner Notification★	Winners are notified in February.
Awards★	Five winners receive a $1,500 prize, a Camp $tart-Up scholarship, and many other prizes.

Advice★

Be sure to submit three copies of the business plan with the application. There are great tips for developing a business plan on the Web site.

Competition★	**BOOK IT! National Reading Incentive Program**
Sponsor★	Pizza Hut, BOOK IT! P.O. Box 2999 Wichita, KS 67201
Web Address★	http://www.bookitprogram.com
Area★	Language arts
Competition Origin★	1985
Purpose★	To develop a lifelong love of reading in children.
Description★	Students in participating classes meet reading goals as established by the classroom teacher to win prizes. Teachers can request guidelines from the sponsor year-round, and they are also available on the Web site.
Eligibility★	Students in grades K–6.
Important Dates★	The program usually begins in early October and runs through the end of March. See guidelines for specific dates.
How to Enter★	Talk to your classroom teacher or principal.
Judging Criteria★	Teachers set monthly reading goals, which may vary from month to month. Goals may include the numbers of books read, number of pages or chapters read, number of minutes spent reading, and so forth.
Judges★	Classroom teacher sets the goals.
Winner Notification★	Everyone wins. Each classroom teacher may handle awards differently.
Awards★	There are a variety of awards given such as posters, cutouts, fun reading activities, family involvement, and pizza awards.
Advice★	Be sure to discuss this early with your teacher or school principal.

Competition★	**Botball Robotics**
Sponsor★	KISS Institute for Practical Robotics 1818 W. Lindsey, Bldg. D, Ste. 100 Norman, OK 73069
Web Address★	http://www.botball.org/about_botball/index.html
Areas★	Engineering, mathematics, science, and technology
Competition Origin★	2000
Purpose★	To promote hands-on experience in science, technology, engineering, and math.
Description★	Students in 5–10-member teams design, build, and program a robot. The Web site has all the information needed to join or start a team.
Eligibility★	Students in grades 6–12.
Important Dates★	Schools should register by early December to receive a discount; otherwise, register 2 weeks prior to your regional tournament. Botball regional tournaments are held February through May. See guidelines for specific dates.
How to Enter★	Students may register online through the Web site.
Judging Criteria★	Students are judged according to use of robotics equipment, attendance during teacher tutorials, number of students participating, and future plans for funding of the robot.
Judges★	Volunteers, sponsors, and mentors in each region.
Winner Notification★	Winners are announced at each tournament.
Awards★	Various awards and scholarships are given to the winners of this competition, dependent upon region and sponsorship.
Advice★	This is an expensive, team-based competition. Visit the Web site to find out if there is a team in your area.

Competition★	**Christopher Columbus Awards**
Sponsor★	Christopher Columbus Fellowship Foundation 110 Genesee St., Ste. 390 Auburn, NY 13021
Web Address★	http://www.christophercolumbusawards.com
Areas★	Creativity/problem solving, science, service learning, and technology
Competition Origin★	1996
Purpose★	To encourage students' curiosity and creativity in order to help them improve their community through scientific and technological innovation.
Description★	Students compete in groups of three to four people with an adult coach. The teams have to identify a problem in their community and create a solution. Guidelines can be obtained through the Web site.
Eligibility★	Students in grades 6–8.
Important Dates★	The deadline for entry is mid-February. See guidelines for specific dates.
How to Enter★	The coach must register the teams online through the Web site.
Judging Criteria★	Students are judged on their creativity, innovation, scientific accuracy, feasibility, and communication.
Judges★	The sponsor selects judges from the fields of science and technology.
Winner Notification★	Winners are notified in mid-April.
Awards★	Every team that enters receives a certificate and judges' comments. Thirty semifinalist teams receive a T-shirt. Eight finalist teams receive an all-expenses-paid trip to Walt Disney World and a $200 developmental grant. The two gold medal teams receive a $2,000 U.S. Savings Bond and plaque for each team member and the sponsoring school. The winning team receives a $25,000 grant.
Advice★	Competition guides for coaches and students can be downloaded from the Web site.

Competition★	The Clarke-Bradbury International Science Fiction Competition
Sponsor★	The European Space Agency's (ESA) Technology Transfer and Promotion Office (ESA-TTP) as part of its ongoing project—"Innovative Technologies in Science Fiction for Space Applications (ITSF)." All information regarding the contest is available online only.
Web Address★	http://www.itsf.org
Areas★	Language arts and visual arts
Competition Origin★	2003
Purpose★	To promote innovative ideas for future space technologies; recognize and pursue viable space technologies found in science fiction; provide a link between young writers and the space community; encourage young people to read and write science fiction; and share the ingenuity and creativity of young minds with the general public.
Description★	Participants write a science fiction story and/or develop a creative a piece of artwork. Entries must incorporate the topic provided. Visit the Web site for guidelines.
Eligibility★	Space and science fiction enthusiasts from all nations between 15 and 30 years of age.
Important Dates★	Entries must be submitted by late February. See guidelines for specific dates.
How to Enter★	Complete the entry form at the Web address and mail it to the sponsor.
Judging Criteria★	The jury makes decisions based upon convincing use of technology in the story; innovative ideas and the ability to think "outside the box"; development of storyline, plot, and characters; clarity of expression, style, and degree of realism; and convincing depiction of events.
Judges★	A jury of scientists and writers appointed by the sponsors.
Winner Notification★	Winners are announced at a special ceremony honoring the contestants at Noreascon, a science fiction convention, in September.

★ ★

Awards★

The winner in each category receives $600, and the runners-up in each category receive $300. They also receive complementary copies of the ESA brochure on Innovative Technologies from Science Fiction, as well as two other ESA publications. The winner is invited to attend and present his or her story at the ITSF session of the International Astronautical Federation Congress.

Competition★	**Congressional Art Competition**
Sponsor★	United States House of Representatives Washington, DC 20515
Web Address★	http://www.house.gov
Area★	Visual arts
Competition Origin★	1980
Purpose★	To afford students the opportunity to express their creativity and to share these creative talents with the community.
Description★	Students first submit artwork based upon a particular theme at the congressional district level, with winners moving onto compete at the national level. Contact your local congressional representative for guidelines.
Eligibility★	Students in grades 9–12.
Important Dates★	Congressional competitions are announced in the fall and held in the spring. See guidelines for specific dates.
How to Enter★	Guidelines and entry forms are available from your local congressional representative.
Judging Criteria★	Artwork is judged on creativity.
Judges★	Art and art education experts.
Winner Notification★	Local dates vary, but national competition winners are notified in late spring/early summer.
Awards★	All students receive a certificate signed by a member of Congress. At the district level, winning artwork is displayed for a year in local offices of Congress members. At the national level, winning artwork is displayed for a year in the Cannon Tunnel.

★ ★

Competition★	**Continental Mathematics League**
Sponsor★	Continental Mathematics League P.O. Box 2196 St. James, NY 11780-0605
Web Address★	http://www.continentalmathleague.hostrack.com
Area★	Mathematics
Competition Origin★	1980
Purpose★	To enhance students' mathematical problem solving skills.
Description★	Meets are held throughout the year, featuring different questions per meet and division. Guidelines may be obtained on the Web site or by writing to the sponsor.
Eligibility★	Students in grades 2–9.
Important Dates★	Register by early October. Meets are held throughout the school year. See guidelines for specific dates.
How to Enter★	Register by contacting the sponsor.
Judging Criteria★	Accuracy of answers.
Judges★	Judges are appointed for each division meet.
Winner Notification★	Winners are notified in the spring.
Awards★	Medals and certificates are awarded to the winners.

Competition★	**Craftsman/NSTA Young Inventors Awards**
Sponsor★	National Science Teachers Association 1840 Wilson Blvd. Arlington, VA 22201-3000
Web Address★	http://www.nsta.org/programs/craftsman
Areas★	Science and technology
Competition Origin★	1996
Purpose★	This program challenges students to use creativity along with science, technology, and mechanics in order to invent or improve a tool.
Description★	Students send in the completed application form (signed by the student, parent, and teacher-advisor), an Inventor's Log (must be 3–7 pages in length), diagram of the tool, and a photograph of the student demonstrating the tool. Guidelines may be obtained on the Web site or by writing to the sponsor.
Eligibility★	Students in grades 2–8.
Important Dates★	Entries are due in mid-March. See guidelines for specific dates.
How to Enter★	An entry form and list of materials may be downloaded from the Craftsman/NSTA Young Inventors Awards Web site.
Judging Criteria★	Judges are looking for an innovative and creative tool that can actually be put to use.
Judges★	Appointed by the sponsor.
Winner Notification★	Winning students are notified in May.
Awards★	Certificates of appreciation and a small gift are awarded to all participating students. Two national winners receive a $10,000 U.S. Savings Bond. Ten national finalists receive a $5,000 U.S. Savings Bond. Twelve second-place winners receive a $500 U.S. Savings Bond. Twelve third-place winners receive $250 U.S. Savings Bonds.
Advice★	Students can look at past winners' tools on the Web site.

Competition★	**Creative Writing Essay Contest**
Sponsor★	Modern Woodmen of America Attn: Fraternal Department Youth Division P.O. Box 2005 Rock Island, IL 61204-2005
Web Address★	http://www.modern-woodmen.org
Area★	Language arts
Competition Origin★	1986
Purpose★	To provide students with an opportunity to demonstrate their skills in thinking and writing, and to provide experience in an activity of value in both personal and community life.
Description★	Local schools and Modern Woodmen of America representatives sponsor an essay writing contest based upon a theme. A 500-word essay is required. Contact sponsor for guidelines.
Eligibility★	Students in grades 5–12.
Important Dates★	The contest can be held any time from September through June. The due date will be set by the principal or teachers of the participating school. Please order materials 1 month prior to the event. See guidelines for specific dates.
How to Enter★	Contact local sponsor.
Judging Criteria★	Participants may receive: 20 points for creativity (presentation of idea, imagination, color, rhythm, flow, and theme), 20 points for material organization (subject adherence, punctuation, grammar, vocabulary, logic, and subject content), and 10 points for overall effectiveness (appeal, impression, and effect).
Judges★	Civic leaders.
Winner Notification★	Varies with school.
Awards★	Each participating child earns a ribbon. Winners and their schools receive trophies.

Competition★	*Cricket League* Contests
Sponsor★	The *Cricket* Magazine Group P.O. Box 300 Peru, IL 61354
Web Address★	http://www.cricketmag.com
Areas★	Language arts and visual arts
Competition Origin★	1973
Purpose★	To encourage readers' literary and artistic creativity and to provide a forum for personal expression.
Description★	Topics are drawn from issues of *Cricket* Magazine. Stories must be 350 words or fewer. All work must be original, without help from anyone. Contests are found in each issue of the magazine and on its Web site.
Eligibility★	Students ages 9–14.
Important Dates★	This is a monthly contest with entries due by the 25th of each month.
How to Enter★	Entries should be mailed to *Cricket* Magazine Group.
Judging Criteria★	Stories, poems, art, and photography are judged for their technique, originality, and adherence to contest themes and guidelines.
Judges★	Members of *Cricket*'s editorial and art departments.
Winner Notification★	Winners are notified approximately 1 month after entry deadline.
Awards★	Eight to 15 winning entries (depending on space available) are published in two age categories (10 and under and 11 and up) 3 months after the issue in which the contest description appeared. The winning essays are also published on the magazine's Web site.
Advice★	Do not e-mail or fax submissions. Only one entry per person is allowed each month.

Competition★	Discover Card Tribute Award Scholarships
Sponsor★	American Association of School Administrators 801 N. Quincy St., Ste. 700 Arlington, VA 22203-1730
Web Address★	http://www.aasa.org/awards_and_scholarships/discover
Areas★	Leadership and service learning
Competition Origin★	1991
Purpose★	To award scholarships in recognition of high school juniors who exhibit excellence in many areas of their lives beyond academics.
Description★	Scholarships are given for education or training beyond high school. They can be used for course-work, certificate trade schools, and associate or bachelor degrees. Guidelines are available September through December of each year. Applications are sent to all schools, so check with your guidance counselor.
Eligibility★	Students in grade 11 (must carry at least a 2.75 GPA during 9th and 10th grades).
Important Dates★	Applications are due in early January. See guidelines for specific dates.
How to Enter★	Check with your guidance counselor, write to sponsor for an application or request one from the Web site above.
Judging Criteria★	Tribute Award winners are selected on the basis of each student's application package. In addition to their academic achievements, winners must demonstrate outstanding accomplishments in special talents, leadership, obstacles overcome, and community service. Since all criteria areas are judged on an equal basis, winners must show outstanding accomplishments in each area. Judges are looking for the best all-around applicants.
Judges★	Judging is conducted at state and national level with representatives from business, education, and community sectors.
Winner Notification★	Winners are notified in May with letters to the student, principal, and superintendent.

Awards ★

There are two levels of Tribute Award scholarships: State (and District of Columbia) Scholarships: up to 9 Awards at $2,500 each; and National Scholarships: up to 9 Awards at $25,000 each.

Competition★	**Discovery Channel Young Scientist Challenge**
Sponsor★	DiscoverySchool.com 7700 Wisconsin Ave. Bethesda, MD 20814
Web Address★	http://school.discovery.com/sciencefaircentral/dysc
Area★	Science
Competition Origin★	1999
Purpose★	To encourage understanding and exploration in the field of science.
Description★	Based on individual science projects, winners are selected at the regional level to participate in teams completing different scientific challenges. Guidelines can be obtained on the Web site in February.
Eligibility★	Students in grades 5–8.
Important Dates★	Submissions are due in early June. See guidelines for specific dates.
How to Enter★	Students can enter on the Web site.
Judging Criteria★	At the regional level, students are judged for the scientific merit of their work, and more importantly, for their ability to communicate their ideas. National participants are judged on teamwork, communication, leadership, and scientific problem solving.
Judges★	Scientists and teachers appointed at regional and national levels.
Winner Notification★	Winners are notified in September.
Awards★	All finalists receive a trip to Washington, DC, a T-shirt, $50 gift certificate, plaque, and a medal. The first-place winner receives a $20,000 cash prize, second place receives a $10,000 cash prize, third place receives a $5,000 cash prize, and a $500 cash prize is awarded to places 4th to 40th.
Advice★	The Web site has lots of great ideas for science students and projects.

Competition★	**Donna Reed Festival for the Performing Arts**
Sponsor★	The Donna Reed Foundation for the Performing Arts 1305 Broadway Denison, IA 51442
Web Address★	http://www.donnareed.org
Area★	Performing arts
Competition Origin★	1987
Purpose★	To support talented individuals who desire to pursue an education or career in the performing arts.
Description★	Based on level of talent, applicants submit audio or videotapes of their work; recommendations from teachers or professionals; and a statement from the applicant about his or her plans and future goals in performing arts. Guidelines are available on the Web site.
Eligibility★	Students in grade 12 who are qualified to enter an undergraduate college program.
Important Dates★	Application deadline is in March. Notification to finalists is in mid-April. The Donna Reed Festival of Workshops and live competition is in mid-June. See guidelines for specific dates.
Judging Criteria★	Overall performance is considered with different criteria for each division (acting, musical, theater, and vocal).
Judges★	Judges are selected from the head or chairmanship of performing arts departments (music, dance, theater, writing, communications, etc.) from major colleges, as well as practicing professionals in the various disciplines (symphony conductors, chorus directors, directors of theater companies, etc.).
Winner Notification★	Winners are notified in mid-June.
Awards★	Three $4,000 scholarships in each division and six $500 scholarships in each division. Eight full-tuition, all-expenses-paid scholarships to the Donna Reed Festival of Workshops in June are also awarded.

Competition★	**Doors to Diplomacy**
Sponsor★	GlobalSchoolNet sponsors the Web site on behalf of the U.S. Department of State. This is an electronically-based competition.
Web Address★	http://www.globalschoolnet.org/gsh/doors
Areas★	Social studies and technology
Competition Origin★	2003
Purpose★	To encourage middle school and high school students around the world to produce Web projects that teach others about the importance of international affairs and diplomacy.
Description★	Doors to Diplomacy is a collaborative project, where small teams are formed consisting of two to five student members and up to two adult coaches. Research can be conducted both online and offline, and then the findings are assembled to produce an educational Web site. Students are also encouraged to become spokespersons for their projects. Visit the Web site for competition details, suggestions, and former projects.
Eligibility★	Students in grades 6–12.
Important Dates★	Register between October and February. See guidelines for specific dates.
How to Enter★	Students can register online.
Judging Criteria★	The peer review rubric evaluates theme, content, organization, conventions, appearance, and technical elements. The rubric can be viewed on the Web site.
Judges★	There is a peer review process for this competition. Additionally, the Doors to Diplomacy International Review Board is comprised of distinguished Internet and education professionals, who are selected based on their experience and devotion to online collaborative learning, and their reputation as visionaries of the Global Information Infrastructure.
Winner Notification★	Winners are notified in May.
Awards★	Each student team member of the winning Doors to Diplomacy Award team receives a $2,000 scholarship, and the winning coaches' schools each receive a $500 cash award. The State Department also spon-

sors a trip to Washington, DC, where the winners receive a private tour of the State Department facilities, meet with key officials, and participate in a special award presentation ceremony. Each team that submits a completed project receives a special Doors to Diplomacy certificate.

Advice★

The Web site contains lots of helpful information.

★ ★

Competition★	**DuPont Challenge Science Essay Awards Program**
Sponsor★	General Learning Corporation 900 Skokie Blvd., Ste. 200 Northbrook, IL 60062-4028
Web Address★	http://www.glcomm.com/Dupont
Areas★	Engineering, language arts, mathematics, and science
Competition Origin★	2000
Purpose★	To promote student interest in all avenues of science.
Description★	The DuPont Challenge is an opportunity for students to write an essay of 700–1,000 words discussing a scientific development, event, or theory that has captured their interest and attention. Contact the sponsor for guidelines.
Eligibility★	Students in grades 7–12.
Important Dates★	Entries due by mid-January. See guidelines for specific dates.
How to Enter★	Complete the entry form on the Web site and submit it with an original essay.
Judging Criteria★	An appropriate choice of subject matter; thorough research using a variety of resource materials; careful consideration of how the subject matter affects you and humankind; and a clear, well organized writing style that has been proofed for spelling and grammatical errors are judged. In a winning essay, creativity, originality, and style are important, as are a neat presentation, the quality of scientific research, good writing, and careful attention to spelling, grammar, and punctuation.
Judges★	DuPont appoints judges.
Winner Notification★	Winners are notified by the sponsor following competition deadlines and judging.
Awards★	The program awards educational prizes totaling more than $13,000. Three winners and 24 honorable mentions are awarded in each of the two divisions: junior division (grades 7–9) and senior division (grades 10–12). Winners in each division receive these cash awards: first place, $1,500; four finalists, $500 each; honorable mention, $50 each. The first-place winner in each division will be flown

Advice★

to NASA's Johnson Space Center in Houston, along with a parent and the sponsoring science and English teachers as special guests. Airfare and hotel expenses will be paid by DuPont.

Before you begin to research and write, read the winning essays on the Web site and carefully review the student competition rules.

Competition★	**The Elvis Week Annual Art Contest and Exhibit**
Sponsor★	The Elvis Week Annual Art Exhibit and Contest Graceland Division of Elvis Presley Enterprises, Inc. P.O. Box 16508 3734 Elvis Presley Blvd. Memphis, TN 38186-0508
Web Address★	http://www.elvis.com
Area★	Visual arts
Competition Origin★	1984
Purpose★	To provide artists the opportunity to express their feelings and ideas about the rock 'n' roll legend, Elvis Presley.
Description★	The art exhibit and contest offers four judged categories, as well as two exhibit only categories. Judged categories are: Craft Division, Non-Professional Art Division, Professional Art Division, and Photography Division. The exhibit-only categories are: Youth Art Division (for ages 16 and under) and Special Division (for disabled artists). Artists who enter the Youth or Special Division may also enter one or more of the other categories. There is no charge to enter the contest. Visit the Web site for guidelines.
Eligibility★	The Youth Art Division is open to all students ages 16 and under.
Important Dates★	Entries are due in late July. Artwork is on display (no admission charge) at Graceland in August. Judging for the competition categories is in early August. See guidelines for specific dates.
How to Enter★	For complete rules and entry form, contact sponsor.
Judging Criteria★	See guidelines for details.
Judges★	A panel of judges from the Memphis community.
Winner Notification★	Winners, if not present, will be notified by mail.
Awards★	Winners of the judged categories will receive ribbons and token of appreciation. Each entrant of the Youth and Special Divisions will receive a certificate along with a token of appreciation.

Advice★

All art must be the original work of the exhibitors (copies are not accepted) and must relate to the image of Elvis Presley or his home, Graceland.

Competition★	**Executive Women International Scholarship Program (EWISP)**
Sponsor★	Executive Women International 515 S. 700 East, Ste. 2A Salt Lake City, UT 84102
Web Address★	http://www.executivewomen.org
Area★	Academic recognition
Competition Origin★	1974
Purpose★	To encourage, motivate, and assist high school juniors to develop career objectives and provide financial support.
Description★	Students can compete at the local chapter level and at the national level. Students must complete a student application form, obtain a personal and teacher endorsement, and submit an autobiographical essay as outlined in the application. Guidelines are available through the local chapter scholarship chair. Chapter addresses and Web sites are located on the Web site.
Eligibility★	Students in grade 11 who live in areas serviced by an EWI chapter whose career plans include a 4-year degree in any business or professional field of study.
Important Dates★	Deadlines vary from chapter to chapter. See guidelines for specific dates.
How to Enter★	Application materials can be obtained through local chapters. Students need a recommendation from a sponsoring teacher and community member.
Judging Criteria★	Judging is based on application materials and the following criteria: scholastic achievement, extra-curricular activities, leadership, dependability, communication skills, and good citizenship.
Judges★	Representatives of the business, education, and civic sectors.
Winner Notification★	Chapter EWISP chairs notify winners.
Awards★	Each participating chapter gives scholarship awards of varying amounts. National corporate awards are: first place, $10,000; second place, $6,000; third place, $4,000; and five finalists, $2,000 each.

★ ★

Advice★

Students should submit their applications through local chapters, as submitting entries to the corporate office creates delays. There are chapters across the United States. Check the Web site to find the chapter nearest you.

Competition★	**The Explorers Club Youth Activity Fund**
Sponsor★	The Explorers Club Youth Activity Fund 46 E. 70th St. New York, NY 10021
Web Address★	http://explorers.org/grants/youthfund.php
Area★	Science
Competition Origin★	1904
Purpose★	To help foster a new generation of explorers and to build a reservoir of young men and women dedicated to the advancement of knowledge of the world by probing the unknown through field research.
Description★	Grants may be requested to cover investigations anywhere in the world. Applicants must provide a brief, but knowledgeable explanation of the proposed project in their own words and two letters of recommendation. The awards will be used to support fieldwork or closely related endeavors. Transportation, supplies, subsistence, and equipment are appropriate, but salaries and expenses such as tuition or indirect costs are not. Joint funding is strongly encouraged and applicants should list other sources of funds. Grantees are expected to submit a report/essay with an itemized statement of expenses at the end of the project. Photographs are particularly encouraged. Guidelines may be obtained on the Web site or by writing to the sponsor.
Eligibility★	Students in grades 9–12 and college undergraduates.
Important Dates★	Deadline for applications is mid-February. See guidelines for specific dates.
How to Enter★	Contact sponsor or download an application form from the Web site.
Judging Criteria★	A knowledgeable explanation of the project and two letters of recommendation.
Judges★	Appointees of The Explorers Club.
Winner Notification★	Winners are notified at the end of May.
Awards★	Although there is no strict limit, grants typically are in the range of $500 to $1,500. In some cases grants will be co-funded by local chapters of The Explorers Club.

Only a limited number of applicants from a single institution can expect to be funded in any year.

Advice★

Projects must be carried out under supervision of a qualified scientist. Applicants are encouraged to seek other sources of funding in addition to this grant.

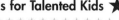

Competition★	FedChallenge
Sponsor★	Federal Reserve Bank of Boston 600 Atlantic Ave. Boston, MA 02210
Web Address★	http://www.bos.frb.org/education/fedchallenge
Area★	Social studies
Competition Origin★	1995
Purpose★	To encourage economic literacy by allowing students to analyze economic conditions.
Description★	At regional and district level, each team, consisting of five students, presents an analysis of the current state of the economy and a monetary policy recommendation for the Federal Open Market Committee (FOMC). Following the presentation, judges question each team about their presentation and their knowledge of macroeconomic theory. One team per participating Federal Reserve District competes at the national competition in Washington, DC. Guidelines can be obtained on the Web site.
Eligibility★	Students in grades 9–12.
Important Dates★	Preliminary rounds of competition are held in late March. The District Championships are held in mid-April, and the National Competition is held in early May. See guidelines for specific dates.
How to Enter★	Teachers can register teams online.
Judging Criteria★	Knowledge of the Federal Reserve, monetary policy, and current economic conditions; response to judges' questions; quality of research, analysis, and presentation; and teamwork.
Judges★	Federal Reserve Bank economists and officers judge the district competitions. FOMC members—Federal Reserve Governors and Reserve Bank Presidents—judge the national finals.
Winner Notification★	Winners are notified on-site at each level.
Awards★	The district champions travel to Washington, DC, at the expense of the local Reserve Bank for the national competition. Citibank has established scholarships and grants for teams at the national level.

Advice★

The Web site has a great set of Frequently Asked
Questions (FAQs).

Competition★	Federal Junior Duck Stamp Program
Sponsor★	U.S. Fish and Wildlife Service The Federal Duck Stamp Program 4401 North Fairfax Dr. Mail-Stop: MBSP 4070 Arlington, VA 22203-1622
Web Address★	http://duckstamps.fws.gov/junior/junior.htm
Areas★	Science and visual arts
Competition Origin★	1989
Purpose★	To teach wetlands awareness and conservation through the arts to students.
Description★	The JDS program is a curriculum-based art education program One of the activities suggested in the curriculum guide is designing a Junior Duck Stamp—a stamp that is sold by the Wildlife Service every year—and entering that design in the state JDS contest. Information is mailed to schools in October. Teachers may write to the sponsor for a free curriculum guide and a JDS video. Visit the Web site for more details.
Eligibility★	Students in grades K–12.
Important Dates★	Contact the state sponsor as dates vary. Alternatively, visit the Web site and look for your state's deadlines.
How to Enter★	Mail your design to your state sponsor.
Judging Criteria★	Accurate depiction of wildlife in its natural habitat.
Judges★	Each state selects five judges.
Winner Notification★	Winners are notified in November.
Awards★	The U.S. Fish and Wildlife Service awards a certificate of participation to each student who enters a design, 100 ribbons across all age categories, and a state Best of Show ribbon. In some states, sponsors may offer additional prizes. The national first-, second-, and third-place winners, their art teachers, and one of their parents win a free trip to Washington, DC, to attend the Federal Duck Stamp Contest. The first-place winner also receives a $2,500 award, and his or her design is used to create a Federal Junior Duck Stamp.
Advice★	Download the competition rules and entry forms from the Web site.

Competition★	**Fire Fighting Home Robot Contest**
Sponsor★	Trinity College Fire Fighting Robot Contest 190 Mohegan Dr. West Hartford, CT 06117
Web Address★	http://www.trincoll.edu/events/robot
Area★	Technology
Competition Origin★	1994
Purpose★	To build a computer-controlled robot that can find and extinguish a fire in a house.
Description★	Students of all ages build computer-controlled, programmed robots that perform a necessary function in the home. Guidelines may be obtained on the Web site or by writing to the sponsor.
Eligibility★	Anyone of any age or ability. The contest is open to groups or individuals.
Important Dates★	The annual competition is held in late spring. See guidelines for specific dates.
How to Enter★	Contact the sponsor.
Judging Criteria★	The capability of the robot to quickly find and extinguish a fire in a house.
Judges★	University-appointed judges.
Winner Notification★	Winners are announced at the competition.
Awards★	There are cash prizes for the top robots in each division. There are also non-cash prizes given and these vary each year.
Advice★	Get the rules and start working early. You can also see pictures of previous winning robots on the Web site.

Competition★	**Freedoms Foundation National Awards Program**
Sponsor★	Freedoms Foundation at Valley Forge 1601 Valley Forge Valley Forge, PA 19482-0706
Web Address★	http://www.freedomsfoundation.com/national.asp
Area★	Language arts
Competition Origin★	1949
Purpose★	To publicly honor and recognize the exceptional efforts of individuals, organizations, corporations, and schools who promote, through words or deeds, an understanding of responsible citizenship and the benefits of a free society.
Description★	Most youth category entries are in the form of written essays and speeches. However, projects for individual achievement or involvement in communities are also welcome. Eligible material must have been written, developed, or released during the awards year. Guidelines are available year-round on the Web site or by contacting the sponsor.
Eligibility★	Students in grades K–12.
Important Dates★	Deadline for entries is in June. See guidelines for specific dates.
How to Enter★	Submit a typed copy of essay or speech. Activities should be put in a ring binder, photo album, or scrapbook with substantiating materials.
Judging Criteria★	A nomination must relate to one or more of the basic American rights set forth in the *American Credo* or the obligations outlined in the *Bill of Responsibilities*, both of which are Freedom Foundation documents available from the sponsor.
Judges★	National Awards Jury is comprised of chief and associate State Supreme Court justices and executive officers from National Veteran Service and civic clubs, veterans, or educational organizations.
Winner Notification★	Winners are notified in the fall.
Awards★	Top recipient in the Youth Category receives $100 U.S. Savings Bond and framed George Washington Honor Medal. All other recipients receive a George Washington Honor Medal.

Advice★

Winning entries from other local/national contests are eligible. Entries may not be the product of class-room assignments.

Competition★	**Future City Competition**
Sponsor★	National Engineers Week Future City Competition 1420 King St. Alexandria, VA 22314
Web Address★	http://www.futurecity.org
Areas★	Engineering, mathematics, and science
Competition Origin★	1984
Purpose★	To promote interests in math, science, and engineering by providing an engineering challenge that is hands-on as students create their city for the future.
Description★	Students use special software to design a city and presentation, along with writing an essay. Guidelines may be obtained on the Web site or by writing to the sponsor.
Eligibility★	Students in grades 7–8.
Important Dates★	Competition materials are mailed in mid-August. Regional competitions end in late January. The national competition is held in mid-February. See guidelines for specific dates.
How to Enter★	Teams of students must register on the Web site.
Judging Criteria★	Students are judged on computerized design, physical model, essay, and verbal presentation.
Judges★	Engineers and teachers appointed by the regional and national coordinators.
Winner Notification★	Winners are announced on-site at regional and national levels.
Awards★	The first-place winner receives a trip to U.S. Space Camp in Huntsville, Alabama. The first runner-up receives up to $2,000 in scholarships for his or her school's technology program. A second runner-up also receives $1,000 in scholarships for his or her school's technology program.
Advice★	Teams need an engineer mentor to assist with projects.

Competition★	**Future Problem Solving Program**
Sponsor★	Future Problem Solving Program 2028 Regency Road Lexington, KY 40503-2309
Web Address★	http://www.fpsp.org
Areas★	Creativity/problem solving and language arts
Competition Origin★	1974
Purpose★	To motivate and assist students to develop and use creative thinking skills; learn about complex issues that will shape the future; develop an active interest in the future; develop and use written and verbal communication skills; learn and utilize problem solving strategies; develop and use teamwork skills; develop and use research skills; and develop and use critical and analytical thinking skills.
Description★	The regular program consists of teams of four given a futuristic "fuzzy" situation with which they must brainstorm problems, identify an underlying problem, brainstorm solutions to that problem, set criteria for judging the solutions, rank the top solutions, and pick the best solution. The individual program is a scaled down version of the regular program, consisting of just one participant. The scenario writing program has participants write short stories on designated topics taking place in the future. The community problem solving program has a team of any size identify a real life problem, follow the regular program steps to a best solution, and finally implement its solution. Contact the Future Problem Solving Program for guidelines.
Eligibility★	Students in grades 4–12. There are three grade divisions: Junior (4–6); Intermediate (7–9); and Senior (10–12).
Important Dates★	Each state has its own deadlines for when the problems are due. For the Open Division, the qualifying problem is due by mid-March. The International Conference is held during the second weekend in June. See guidelines for specific dates.
How to Enter★	Contact the Future Problem Solving Program or visit the Web site.

Judging Criteria★

Contact the sponsor for information on judging criteria.

Judges★

Evaluators for the International Conference are nominated by their state affiliate directors and chosen from a pool of all of those who are nominated.

Winner Notification★

Winners are announced at the competition.

Awards★

The awards for winning the various competitions vary from state to state. The norm includes trophies and/or plaques. Winners at the International Conference are also awarded trophies and/or plaques.

Advice★

To achieve the highest possible scores, participants are advised to utilize the practice problems, research the topic thoroughly, and keep an open mind for all possible solutions to their problem.

Competition★	**George S. and Stella M. Knight Essay Contest**
Sponsor★	The National Society of the Sons of the American Revolution 1000 S. 4th St. Louisville, KY 40203
Web Address★	http://www.sar.org/youth/knightrl.htm
Areas★	Language arts and social studies
Competition Origin★	1988
Purpose★	The contest is designed to give high school students an opportunity to explore events that shaped American history.
Description★	The contest is for an original, researched, and proven topic written in English. The topic of the essay shall deal with: an event, person, philosophy, or ideal associated with the American Revolution; the Declaration of Independence; or the framing of the United States Constitution. Students must cite at least five references with the minimum of three being printed references. References from encyclopedias or all electronic references will not be accepted as source material and will cause the essay to be disqualified. The essay must have a minimum of 750 words and not exceed 1,000 words excluding title page, footnotes, bibliography, and biography. Contact local affiliates or visit the national Web site for guidelines.
Eligibility★	Students in grades 11–12.
Important Dates★	State affiliates should be contacted for local dates.
How to Enter★	The contest must be entered through a Chapter of the Sons of the American Revolution near the student's residence.
Judging Criteria★	Essays are judged on the following criteria: historical accuracy; clarity of thought; organization and proven topic; grammar and spelling; and documentation.
Judges★	Local, state, and national judges are appointed by the SAR.
Winner Notification★	Winners are notified by state chapters upon completion of competition, and national winners are notified prior to Annual Congress.

Awards★

State and Chapter prizes vary. The National Society awards are: first place, $3,000, a winning recognition plaque, and airfare and hotel for 2 nights at the SAR Annual Congress; second place, $2,000; and third place, $1,000. The winning essay of the national contest will be submitted for publication in *The SAR Magazine*.

Competition★	**Graphic Communications Week Poster Contest**
Sponsor★	International Graphic Arts Education Association, Inc. (IGAEA) 1899 Preston White Dr. Reston, VA 20191-4367
Web Address★	http://www.igaea.org
Area★	Visual arts
Competition Origin★	2004
Purpose★	To give students the opportunity to symbolize the power and importance of printed communication through visual art.
Description★	Students design a poster for Graphic Communications Week, which typically revolves around Benjamin Franklin's birthday (January 17). The theme can encompass anything that symbolizes the power and importance of printed communications. Visit the Web site for guidelines.
Eligibility★	Students in grades 6–12.
Important Dates★	Posters must be received by mid-June. See guidelines for specific dates.
How to Enter★	Students can download an application from the Web site. All entries must be mailed to the coordinator for each year's competition (the name and address are printed on the entry form).
Judging Criteria★	Adherence to entry guidelines and a poster that symbolizes the power and importance of printed communications.
Judges★	Appointed by the sponsor.
Winner Notification★	Winners are notified in time for the annual summer conference.
Awards★	$300 for first-place winners, and $100 each for second- and third-place winners. Winning posters are displayed at the annual summer conference.

Competition★	*Guideposts* **Young Writers Contest**
Sponsor★	*Guideposts* Magazine 16 E. 34th St. New York, NY 10016
Web Address★	http://www.guideposts.com/young_writers_contest.asp
Area★	Language arts
Competition Origin★	1965
Purpose★	To promote young people's writing talent and their awareness of how faith plays a part in their everyday lives.
Description★	Students write a true personal story about an experience that deeply touched or changed their lives. Manuscripts must be typed and double-spaced, with a maximum of 1,200 words. Guidelines may be obtained on the Web site or by writing to the sponsor.
Eligibility★	Students in grades 11–12.
Important Dates★	Entries are due in late November. See guidelines for specific dates.
How to Enter★	Follow guidelines as described in the contest announcement on the Web site.
Judging Criteria★	Manuscripts must be brief, first-person stories.
Judges★	*Guideposts* staff.
Winner Notification★	Winners are notified by mail prior to the June announcement placed in *Guideposts*.
Awards★	First prize: $10,000 scholarship; second prize: $8,000 scholarship; third prize: $6,000 scholarship; fourth prize: $4,000 scholarship; fifth prize: $3,000; sixth through tenth prizes: $1,000; and eleventh through 20th prizes: $250 gift certificate.
Advice★	Read contest rules carefully before submitting your story. Keep a copy of your story; only winners can be acknowledged, and manuscripts will not be returned. If you want acknowledgment that your story has been received, include a self-addressed, stamped postcard when you submit it.

Competition★	**Harry Singer Foundation Essay Contests**
Sponsor★	The Harry Singer Foundation P.O. Box 223159 Carmel, CA 93923
Web Address★	http://www.singerfoundation.org
Areas★	Language arts and social studies
Competition Origin★	1987
Purpose★	To encourage the common person's participation in public policy making.
Description★	Students write essays on different topics for different contests. For example, in 2004, topics included society, government, war, elections, and excellence. Guidelines for these contests can be obtained through the Web site.
Eligibility★	Students ages 13–18.
Important Dates★	Check the Web site as the contest dates vary for each one.
How to Enter★	Participants may enter this contest through the Web site or by contacting the sponsor.
Judging Criteria★	The criteria vary, but students should be well read and able to demonstrate conceptual understandings in their essays. Grammar, punctuation, and spelling, as well as presentation, should adhere to conventional standards.
Judges★	Appointed by the Harry Singer Foundation.
Winner Notification★	Winners are notified 6 weeks after each competition deadline.
Awards★	All participants receive certificates and their essays are published online. For each contest, there is a first prize of $200, second prize of $100, and third prize of $75.
Advice★	The competition Web site has detailed instructions and application information that need to be carefully read.

Competition★	HOBY Sophomore Leadership Seminars
Sponsor★	Hugh O'Brian Youth Foundation (HOBY) 10880 Wilshire Blvd., Ste. 410 Los Angeles, CA 90024
Web Address★	http://www.hoby.org
Area★	Leadership
Competition Origin★	1958
Purpose★	To seek out, recognize, and develop leadership potential among high school sophomores and to promote understanding among this group of America's Incentive System.
Description★	Schools select a student who best represents their community's concept of an outstanding sophomore student leader. Contact the sponsor for guidelines.
Eligibility★	Students in grade 10.
Important Dates★	Nomination forms are sent to all high schools in the fall. Forms must have been returned by the high schools to the Los Angeles office for guaranteed acceptance by mid-November. The final deadline for acceptance is the end of February. See guidelines for specific dates.
How to Enter★	Apply to principal and/or guidance counselor.
Judging Criteria★	Prospective students are asked to complete three essay questions on the form: How have you: 1) demonstrated leadership ability? 2) expressed sensitivity and concern for others? 3) shown the desire to learn and share knowledge and experience with others?
Judges★	Each student applicant's school principal or guidance counselor is the judge. A school "selection panel" may also be formed.
Awards★	Upon selection, the student will be allowed to attend one of HOBY's 91 leadership seminars in his or her state free of charge. At this seminar the student will interact with identified leaders in the fields of business, industry, science, arts, education, and government.
Winner Notification★	Notifying the school winner is the responsibility of each school.

Advice★

The vast majority of HOBY's work is done through its 4,000 volunteers across the U.S., Canada, Mexico, and the Bahamas. There is no cost to the student, school, or parent. From each local leadership seminar, one boy and girl are selected to attend HOBY's week long World Leadership Congress (WLC) in July at no cost. The WLC is held in a different city each year and is coordinated by a major university.

Competition★	Idea of America Essay Contest
Sponsor★	National Endowment for the Humanities (NEH) 1100 Pennsylvania Ave. NW Washington, DC 20506
Web Address★	http://www.neh.fed.us/wtp/essay/index.html
Areas★	Language arts and social studies
Competition Origin★	2002
Purpose★	To promote students to think, analyze, and write about important people and events in American history and to also encourage citizenship in young students.
Description★	Students write a 1,200 word essay on specific principles that have helped shape America. Guidelines are available through the Web site.
Eligibility★	Students in grade 11 and homeschool students ages 16–17.
Important Dates★	The deadline for entry is mid-April. See guidelines for specific dates.
How to Enter★	Submit the essay online or by mail.
Judging Criteria★	The judges are looking for a strong understanding of American history, a well-researched topic, original work, and a grammatically correct essay.
Judges★	Appointed by NEH.
Winner Notification★	Winners are notified in the fall.
Awards★	Six national finalists are honored at an awards ceremony in Washington, DC. The winner of the best essay wins $5,000, and the five runners-up each receive $1,000. The winning essay is published in a national forum.

Competition★	**Intel International Science and Engineering Fair**
Sponsor★	Science Service Inc. 1719 N Street N.W. Washington, DC 20036
Web Address★	http://www.sciserv.org/isef
Areas★	Engineering and science
Competition Origin★	1950
Purpose★	To promote science and education by providing a formalized structure for more than 400 affiliated science fairs.
Description★	Students advance from local, regional, state, and national science fairs to compete at the ISEF. Contact your local science fair coordinator or the sponsor for details.
Eligibility★	Students in grades 9–12. Each ISEF affiliated fair may send up to two finalists and one team project to the ISEF.
Important Dates★	Contact sponsor for dates of local, regional, and state fairs. The national fair is held in May each year.
How to Enter★	Complete application and forms as distributed by the sponsor.
Judging Criteria★	Vary with each level of competition.
Judges★	At the national level, judges are international experts from the fields of science, mathematics, and engineering.
Winner Notification★	Winners are announced at the conclusion of each fair.
Awards★	$50,000 in scholarships are given to the top three winners. There is also the opportunity to advance to contests in other countries, and there are several cash awards.
Advice★	Talk to your school's science fair coordinator to get started.

Competition★	**Intel Science Talent Search**
Sponsor★	Science Service 1719 N Street N.W. Washington, DC 20036
Web Address★	http://www.sciserv.org/sts
Areas★	Engineering, mathematics, and science
Competition Origin★	1942
Purpose★	To foster the education of young potential scientists, mathematicians, and engineers.
Description★	Entering high school seniors submit a written report of an independent science, mathematics, or engineering research project. Guidelines are available in mid–August or through the Web site.
Eligibility★	Students entering grade 12.
Important Dates★	Entry materials are available for request in mid-August. Entries must be received by mid-November. See guidelines for specific dates.
How to Enter★	Contact sponsor for official rules and entry form, or obtain an entry form on their Web site.
Judging Criteria★	Evidence of creativity and interest in science.
Judges★	A team of more than 20 judges specializing in a variety of scientific disciplines.
Winner Notification★	In late January, the finalists are notified. The top scholarship winners are notified in March.
Awards★	Three hundred semi-finalists benefit in the following ways: (1) recommendations to colleges and universities for admission and financial assistance; (2) certificates of achievement for students and teachers; and (3) a fine sense of accomplishment and a measure of self–esteem that come from finishing a hard assignment. The 40 finalists, selected from the semi-finalists, are also awarded a trip to Washington, DC, for the 5-day all-expenses-paid Science Talent Institute for final judging and a chance to share $205,000 in scholarships.
Advice★	The research project must be the work of a single individual. Group projects are not eligible.

Competition★	**International Brain Bee**
Sponsor★	Society for Neuroscience University of Maryland School of Dentistry 666 W. Baltimore St. Baltimore, MD 21201-1586
Web Address★	http://web.sfn.org/baw/bee.cfm
Area★	Science
Competition Origin★	2001
Purpose★	To test the neuroscience knowledge of students and to inspire them to pursue careers in the biomedical brain research field.
Description★	Students compete in a question and answer competition. Guidelines can be obtained through the Web site.
Eligibility★	Students in grades 9–12.
Important Dates★	The International Brain Bee is held in mid-March. Local and regional dates may vary. See guidelines for specific dates.
How to Enter★	Contact your local coordinator or visit the Web site for details.
Judging Criteria★	Accuracy of answers.
Judges★	Neuroscientists organize and judge the competition.
Winner Notification★	Winners are announced on-site.
Awards★	The champion receives $3,000, a trip to the Society for Neuroscience annual meeting, an individual trophy, a traveling trophy for his or her high school, and a fellowship to work in the laboratory of a neuroscientist during the summer.
Advice★	The sponsor's Web site includes links to some excellent study resources.

Competition★	International Schools CyberFair
Sponsor★	GlobalSchoolNet. This is an electronically based competition.
Web Address★	http://www.globalschoolnet.org/gsh/cf/index.html
Areas★	Social studies and technology
Competition Origin★	1996
Purpose★	For students, their schools, and their local communities to use the Internet to share resources, establish partnerships, and work together to accomplish common goals.
Description★	An award-winning, authentic learning program used by schools and youth organizations around the world. Students conduct research about their local communities and then publish their findings on the Internet. Recognition is given to schools for the best projects in each of the eight categories: local leaders, businesses, community organizations, historical landmarks, environment, music, art, and local specialties. Visit the Web site for competition details, suggestions, and former projects.
Eligibility★	Students ages 5–19.
Important Dates★	Register between October and March. See guidelines for specific dates.
How to Enter★	Register online. This is a collaborative project, and each team must consist of students and teachers.
Judging Criteria★	The peer review rubric evaluates theme, content, organization, conventions, appearance, and technical elements. Rubrics can be viewed on the Web site.
Judges★	There is a peer review process for this competition. Additionally, candidates for an international Review Board of distinguished Internet and education professionals are selected based on their experience and devotion to online collaborative learning and their reputation as visionaries of the Global Information Infrastructure.
Winner Notification★	Winners are notified in May.
Awards★	Each school or organization that completes a final entry receives a special CyberFair certificate to proudly display in their community. Top projects

receive a 1-year subscription to *Futurist* magazine. Projects that best illustrate "future thinking" are invited to the World Future Society international conference.

★ ★

Competition★	**International Student Media Festival**
Sponsor★	AECT/ISMF 1800 N. Stonelake Drive, Ste. 2 Bloomington, IN 47404
Web Address★	https://www.aect.org/ISMF
Areas★	Technology and visual arts
Competition Origin★	1980
Purpose★	To encourage student media production.
Description★	Students enter a media production in one of the following areas: live action, animation, sequential stills, interactive stills, Web site, photographic essay, and single photograph. Judges are obligated to watch only the first 7 minutes of the entry, but entries can be as long as deemed fit. Guidelines may be obtained on the Web site or by writing to the sponsor.
Eligibility★	Students in grade K–12 and college. There are four grade divisions: K–4; 5–8; 9–12; and college.
Important Dates★	Entries are accepted from March through May. See guidelines for specific dates.
How to Enter★	Write to the sponsor and ask to be placed on the entry form mailing list.
Judging Criteria★	Creativity/originality; organization/purpose; continuity/structure; relevance/importance; use of available resources; clarity; energy/education; residue; technical quality; and general effectiveness.
Judges★	The Association for Educational Communications and Technology.
Winner Notification★	Winners are notified in late July.
Awards★	Students receive certificates and critiques. Winners can also attend an awards ceremony.
Advice★	There are fees that must be submitted with each entry.

Competition★	**Invent America!**
Sponsor★	United States Patent Model Foundation Invent America! P.O. Box 26065 Alexandria, VA 22313
Web Address★	http://www.inventamerica.org
Area★	Science
Competition Origin★	1987
Purpose★	This is a teacher-designed contest created to help students learn through inventing.
Description★	This program allows students to create solutions to unusual problems. Students have to analyze and be creative in solving the problem that is presented. Guidelines are available through the Web site.
Eligibility★	Students in grades K–8.
Important Dates★	Entries are due in mid-June. See guidelines for specific dates.
How to Enter★	Students need to register and order materials through the Web site.
Judging Criteria★	Inventions are judged on creativity, usefulness, illustration, and research methods.
Judges★	A prestigious panel of prominent educators, business leaders, government officials, nationally recognized inventors, scientists, and authors.
Winner Notification★	Winners are notified in the fall.
Awards★	There are first, second, third, and honorable mention prizes awarded for each grade level. The prizes consist of U.S. Savings Bonds and awards certificates.
Advice★	Materials and guidelines for this contest are located on the Web site and may also be used for teaching. Schools must enroll in order for students to participate.

Competition★	**Japan Bowl**
Sponsor★	The Japan-American Society of Washington 1819 L Street, NW, 1B Level Washington, DC 20036
Web Address★	http://www.us-japan.org/dc/education/jbowl.html
Area★	Foreign language
Competition Origin★	1993
Purpose★	To recognize excellence in Japanese language and culture.
Description★	The Japan Bowl is modeled on a quiz show format and aims to make the study of Japanese challenging and enjoyable. Teams of students are asked questions regarding Japanese culture, grammar, kanji, katakana, kotowaza, and onomatopoeic expressions. The winners of the Regional Japan Bowl Competitions are eligible to compete at the National Japan Bowl Competition in Washington, DC. The guidelines can be downloaded from the Web site.
Eligibility★	Students in grades 9–12 who are currently enrolled in Levels II, III, and IV Japanese language classes.
Important Dates★	The national bowl is held in Washington, DC, in March each year. Regional dates vary, so you should check the Web site for the one nearest your school.
How to Enter★	To participate in the Japan Bowl, students must complete and submit the application and agreement forms to their regional Japan Bowl host organization by the specified deadline, which is to be determined by the regional host.
Judging Criteria★	Performance in team and toss-up questions.
Judges★	Appointed by sponsor.
Winner Notification★	Winners are recognized on the day of the bowl, but must be present at the awards ceremony to receive their prizes.
Awards★	Certificates and plaques are given to winning teams. The first-place national winners receive a trip to Japan. Regional awards vary, but those winning at the regional level go on to the national bowl.

Advice★

Sample questions are available on the Web site in the entry requirements and information guide.

Competition★	**John F. Kennedy Profiles in Courage Essay Contest**
Sponsor★	John F. Kennedy Library Profiles in Courage Essay Contest Columbia Point Boston, MA 02125
Web Address★	http://www.jfkcontest.org
Areas★	Language arts and social studies
Competition Origin★	1994
Purpose★	To encourage high school students to write a compelling essay on the meaning of political courage and to learn about and be inspired by America's elected officials, past or present, who have tried to make a difference in the world.
Description★	In fewer than 1,000 words, students write an essay that is original, creative, and demonstrates an understanding of political courage as described by John F. Kennedy in *Profiles in Courage*. Use a variety of sources such as newspaper articles, books, and/or personal interviews to write about one of the following:

1. A current elected public official in the United States who is acting courageously to address a political issue at the local, state, national, or international level.
2. An elected public official in the United States since 1956 who has acted courageously to address a political issue at the local, state, national, or international level.

Visit the Web site for guidelines.

Eligibility★	Students in grades 9–12.
Important Dates★	Entries can be submitted between September and January. See guidelines for specific dates.
How to Enter★	Applications can be downloaded from the Web site. Essays can be submitted online or by mail. Contestants must have a teacher sponsor for guidance and support.
Judging Criteria★	Essays are judged on content (55%) and presentation (45%).

Judges★

A national panel of judges selected by the Kennedy Library.

Winner Notification★

Winners are notified in April.

Awards★

The winner receives $3,000 and is invited to the Kennedy Library in May to accept his or her award. A second-place winner receives $1,000. Five finalists each receive $500. All winners receive a hardcover copy of John F. Kennedy's *Profiles in Courage*. The nominating teacher of the first-place winner is invited to the Kennedy Library in May to receive the John F. Kennedy Public Service Grant in the amount of $500 for school projects encouraging student leadership and civic engagement. All participants receive a certificate of participation.

Competition★	**Joseph S. Rumbaugh Oration Contest**
Sponsor★	The National Society of the Sons of the American Revolution 1000 S. Fourth St. Louisville, KY 40203
Web Address★	http://www.sar.org/youth/rumbaugh.htm
Areas★	Language arts and social studies
Competition Origin★	1945
Purpose★	To bring American history to the high school student and focus on events of today; to draw an intelligent relationship between the past and the present; to clearly demonstrate freedom of opportunity as a basic right of our national heritage; to place a positive emphasis on the plans of our founding fathers; to emphasize justice under law in a free society; and to illustrate how the Revolutionary War influenced our freedom of expression.
Description★	The contest is for an original oration of 5–6 minutes. Topics shall deal with an event within the context of the Revolutionary War and the relationship it bears to America today. Contact your state society or the national office for guidelines. Rules are also available online.
Eligibility★	Students in grades 10–12.
Important Dates★	Dates vary with level of competition. The national entries must be submitted 2 weeks prior to the annual conference. See guidelines for specific dates.
How to Enter★	Participate at the local, state, and district levels.
Judging Criteria★	Composition, delivery, logic, significance, general excellence, and time allocated for delivery are selected criteria.
Judges★	Members of the Sons of the American Revolution.
Winner Notification★	National winners are recognized at the annual Congress on the National Society of the Sons of the American Revolution.

Awards★ National winners receive scholarship awards: first place, $3,000; second place, $2,000; and third place, $1,000. All other finalists win $300. Other national contestants win $200.

Advice★ Contact state sponsor early in the school year.

Competition★	**Kids Are Authors**
Sponsor★	Kids Are Authors Scholastic Book Fairs 1080 Greenwood Blvd. Lake Mary, FL 32746
Web Address★	http://teacher.scholastic.com/activities/kaa
Areas★	Language arts and visual arts
Competition Origin★	1986
Purpose★	To encourage students to interact and cooperate as a team, while at the same time using their reading, writing, and artistic skills.
Description★	Kids Are Authors is a picture book writing and illustration competition. Each entry must be the result of a cooperative effort of three or more students. The winning entry is published in a hardcover edition by Scholastic Books. Guidelines may be obtained on the Web site.
Eligibility★	Students in grades K–8.
Important Dates★	Deadline for entries is mid-March. See guidelines for specific dates.
How to Enter★	Groups of three or more students whose school has held a book fair with Scholastic Book Fairs that school year can enter this competition by writing and illustrating their own, previously unpublished, original picture book. Entries must consist of 8–12 original illustrations, with separate accompanying pages of text with a maximum 50 words per page, typed or handwritten, and no more than 24 total pages. Each entry must be accompanied by a completed official entry form. Write to the address above for more information. Entry forms can also be downloaded from the Web site.
Judging Criteria★	Entries are judged on originality, story content, illustrative quality, and compatibility of text and illustrations.
Judges★	Judges are selected by Scholastic Book Fairs from professionals in the fields of children's literature, art, and education.
Winner Notification★	Winners are notified by the end of May.

Awards★

Two winning schools (one for fiction, one for non-fiction) receive $2,000 in merchandise, framed certificates, medallions, and 100 copies of their published book. Twenty-five honor awards may be selected; honor winners receive $200 in merchandise for their schools and certificates.

Advice★

Start with a group brainstorming session on story ideas. Once the group has come to a consensus on the story line, the children should begin asking themselves what is the best way to express that concept through words and illustrations. Introduce children to various art techniques and allow them to experiment with the one that works best for them. Bold images in bright colors often work best. Project coordinators and students may want to read and review previous Kids Are Authors winners for inspiration.

Competition★	**Kids Philosophy Slam**
Sponsor★	Kids Philosophy Slam P.O. Box 406 Lanesboro, MN 55949
Web Address★	http://www.philosophyslam.org
Areas★	Philosophy and visual arts
Competition Origin★	2000
Purpose★	To give students a voice and encourage them to think using their creative potential through philosophical forums.
Description★	Students use a theme presented by the contest and submit an original piece of work such as a painting, essay, song, or other artwork. Guidelines may be obtained on the Web site or by writing to the sponsor.
Eligibility★	Students in grades K–12.
Important Dates★	Entries should be postmarked by early February. See guidelines for specific dates.
How to Enter★	Make sure to mail your entry to the sponsor.
Judging Criteria★	Creativity, originality, and overall strength of the message the student is conveying. For some competitions, the strength of one's argument is also judged.
Judges★	A panel of philosophers, educators, and parents.
Winner Notification★	Finalists are notified in late March.
Awards★	There are more than $5,000 in prizes, including certificates, T-shirts, and savings bonds awarded.
Advice★	Visit the Web site for resources and ideas.

Competition★	**Knowledge Master Open (KMO)**
Sponsor★	Academic Hallmarks, Inc. P.O. Box 998 Durango, CO 81301
Web Address★	http://www.greatauk.com/KMO.html
Area★	Academic quiz bowl
Competition Origin★	1983
Purpose★	To provide opportunities for all motivated students to participate in a national and international academic competition without the attendant expenses of traveling to a central site and to give students from schools, large or small, urban or rural, a chance to objectively compare their achievement with thousands of the best students in the country's top schools.
Description★	Teams in the Knowledge Master Open receive curriculum-based contest questions (200 at secondary levels; 100 at 5th and 6th grade levels) on a CD-ROM and compete using a computer at their own schools. The event is held twice each year. Up to 4,000 schools and 60,000 students from the U.S. and several foreign countries participate in KMO. Rules from previous competitions are available for the asking or by visiting the Web site. Also, rules and suggestions are sent along with the contest kits. The kits are mailed so that materials arrive at the schools about 10 days in advance of the contest date.
Eligibility★	Students in grades 5–12.
Important Dates★	The elementary KMOs are held in January and March annually. The secondary KMOs take place in December and April. See guidelines for specific dates.
How to Enter★	Academic Hallmarks publishes two free newsletters, the Knowledge Master *Aukxaminer* for elementary competitions and the Knowledge Master *Chronaukles* for the secondary competitions. These are available by writing to Academic Hallmarks. Entry forms are in both of these newsletters. You can also enter online by visiting the KMO Web site.

Judging Criteria★

Accuracy of answers. Winners are those teams in each of the national, state, and enrollment divisions who accumulate the greatest number of points.

Judges★

Self-scoring.

Winner Notification★

Winners are notified the day after the competition.

Awards★

Division winners receive plaques and shirts. All teams receive a poster, stickers for the individual team members, and certificates of participation. All participating schools receive a complete set of results showing the rankings of all teams in the various divisions. A substantial number of top teams are written up in their local newspapers, some have received congratulatory letters from the president, and others have appeared on CNN and NBC.

Advice★

For teams and coaches who have not participated before, it is generally a good idea to become familiar with the format of the event by working with a practice disk. The practice disks are simply the contest disks from previous years. At the end of each KMO, participants are given a special password that turns the contest disk into a practice disk. Teams will benefit by learning to communicate clearly and effectively in the context of the event and to apply various strategies for maximizing their scores.

Competition★	Laws of Life Essay Competition
Sponsor★	John Templeton Foundation 300 Conshohocken State Road, Ste. 500 West Conshohocken, PA 19428
Web Address★	http://www.lawsoflife.org
Area★	Language arts
Competition Origin★	1987
Purpose★	To encourage students to discover values that will help them through life.
Description★	Students are encouraged to write on any topic relating to experiences and people that have shaped their values and lives. Guidelines may be obtained through the Web site.
Eligibility★	Students in grades K–12 and college.
Important Dates★	Local contest dates vary. Check the Web site for contest locations and deadlines.
How to Enter★	Contact the sponsor in order to receive an information kit. This kit includes a manual, teacher's guide, video, Real Player, and other resources.
Judging Criteria★	Students are judged based on compelling content; presentation; and grammar and spelling.
Judges★	Local community members.
Winner Notification★	Winners are announced at the awards ceremony.
Awards★	An awards banquet is held for the contest finalists and their families. Certificates and other awards are presented at the banquet. Local prizes may vary depending on sponsorship.
Advice★	This contest is held locally. There is a section on the Web site that provides guidelines on how to set up and run a contest in your area if there is not one already.

Competition★	**Let's Get Real**
Sponsor★	Let's Get Real 624 Waltonville Rd. Hummelstown, PA 17036
Web Address★	http://www.lgreal.org
Area★	Business
Competition Origin★	2000
Purpose★	This is an opportunity for teams of students to gain experience working on real business problems.
Description★	Students work in teams of two to six members with an adult coordinator, trying to come up with creative solutions to various business problems. The solution is presented in a report format. Finalists are invited to present their solutions in an oral presentation. Guidelines may be obtained on the Web site or by writing to the sponsor.
Eligibility★	Students in grades 6–12.
Important Dates★	Dates vary; see the Web site for specific deadlines.
How to Enter★	An application may be found on the Web site and then mailed or electronically submitted to the sponsor.
Judging Criteria★	This competition is judged on practicality, effectiveness of the solution, cost efficiency, creativity, development of idea, and documentation of the solution.
Judges★	Corporate sponsors.
Winner Notification★	Winners are notified in May.
Awards★	Corporate sponsors offer different challenges and prizes.
Advice★	No individual entries will be considered. Team members may be from the same or different grade levels and may be from the same or different schools. Each team must have at least one adult coordinator.

Competition★	**Letters About Literature Competition**
Sponsor★	The Library of Congress 101 Independence Ave, SE Washington, DC 20540
Web Address★	http://www.loc.gov/loc/cfbook/letters.html
Area★	Language arts
Competition Origin★	1999
Purpose★	To allow students an opportunity to express their personal feelings about a book.
Description★	Students write a letter to an author of their choice explaining how the author's work has changed their way of thinking about the world and themselves. Contact the sponsor for a teacher's guide or download guidelines from the Web site.
Eligibility★	Students in grades 4–12. There are three grade divisions: Level I (4–6); Level II (7–8); and Level III (9–12).
Important Dates★	Letters are due in early December. See guidelines for specific dates.
How to Enter★	Select a book you read recently about which you have strong feelings. You need not like the characters or even the way the events in the book turn out in order to be affected by the story. Write a letter of 750 words or less to the author, explaining what the book taught you about yourself. Make a connection between yourself and a character or an event in the book.
Judging Criteria★	Tone, organization, and expression of personal reaction to the writing.
Judges★	Library of Congress appointees.
Winner Notification★	Winners are notified in April.
Awards★	State winners advance to the national competition and receive cash prizes, plus a $50 Target gift card. Two national winners are selected on each competition level. Target Stores send the six national winners, their parents/guardians, and one of their teachers to Washington, DC, to attend the National Book Festival in the fall. The national winners read their

★ ★

winning letters during the festival and tour sites, and each national winner receives a $500 Target gift card.

Advice★

Do not summarize the plot of the book because the author wrote the story and already knows what happened. What the author doesn't know is the ways in which the book affected you. In other words, think of the audience to whom you are writing—the person who will read the letter. Be honest, personal, and conversational, as if the author were a friend who would write back to you.

Competition★	**The Lions International Peace Poster Contest**
Sponsor★	Lions Clubs International 300 W. 22nd St. Oak Brook, IL 60523-8842
Web Address★	http://www.lionsclubs.org/EN/content/ youth_peace_poster.php3
Area★	Visual Arts
Competition Origin★	1988
Purpose★	To give young people the opportunity to express their thoughts about world peace in an original artwork.
Description★	Posters are judged at the school level and there are two more rounds to reach international competition and the grand prize. Themes change from year to year; for example, the theme for 2005 was "Peace Without Borders." Teachers and principals must contact Lions Clubs International for guidelines. There is also information on the Web site.
Eligibility★	Students ages 11–13.
Important Dates★	Fall deadlines for submitting posters vary according to district, and national deadlines are in early December. See guidelines for specific dates.
How to Enter★	School teachers or principals should contact Lions Clubs International or obtain an application form online. Lions clubs must purchase a competition kit (available in mid-January).
Judging Criteria★	Posters are judged according to originality, artistic merit, and expression of theme.
Judges★	Throughout the judging process, posters are evaluated by different groups of judges. On the international level, they are judged by internationally renowned people involved with art, peace, or children.
Winner Notification★	Winners are announced at each level of competition. International winners are notified at the beginning of February.
Awards★	At the national level there is one grand-prize winner and more than 20 merit finalists. Winning artwork is published on the Web site. Local recognition varies.

Advice★

No one may enter the contest independently. Students and schools must be sponsored by a local Lions club to participate.

Competition★	**Lucent Global Science Scholars Program**
Sponsor★	Lucent Global Science Scholars Program Institute of International Education 809 United Nations Plaza New York, NY 10017
Web Address★	http://www.iie.org/programs/lucent
Areas★	Mathematics, science, and technology
Competition Origin★	1999
Purpose★	To recognize outstanding academic achievements in math, science, and technology.
Description★	Students are chosen based upon high academic performance in math, science, and technology to participate in a Global Summit for researchers. Students may also be eligible for an internship. Guidelines may be obtained on the Web site or by writing to the sponsor.
Eligibility★	Students graduating from grade 12.
Important Dates★	Applications are due the last week in February. See guidelines for specific dates.
How to Enter★	Applications can be downloaded from the Web site.
Judging Criteria★	High academic standing and career plans in science and technology.
Judges★	External screening committees evaluate all written applications by region. The same regional committees read applications and conduct interviews via teleconference.
Winner Notification★	Winners are notified prior to the Summit held in July.
Awards★	Recipients spend a week in Murray Hill, New Jersey, with researchers and scientists and fellow Global Science Scholars at the headquarters of Lucent Technologies and its world-renowned research and development arm, Bell Labs. In addition to attending the Summit, the winning Scholars receive a $5,000 award. If, and when, an appropriate placement can be found, Global Science Scholars are offered internships at a Bell Labs or Lucent Technologies facility.

★ ★

Advice★

Students must demonstrate an interest in pursuing a career in science and technology.

Competition★	**Mandelbrot Competition**
Sponsor★	Greater Testing Concepts The Mandelbrot Group P.O. Box 20534 Stanford, CA 94309-0534
Web Address★	http://www.mandelbrot.org
Area★	Mathematics
Competition Origin★	1990
Purpose★	To introduce high school students to all levels of mathematics while providing stimulating and challenging problems.
Description★	This is a 40-minute math competition that allows for group and individual work. Guidelines can be found on the Web site.
Eligibility★	Students in grades 9–12.
Important Dates★	Contests are administered from October until March. See guidelines for specific dates.
How to Enter★	You may enter this contest by registering on the Web site.
Judging Criteria★	Accuracy of answers.
Judges★	Graded by teachers and coaches.
Winner Notification★	Results are announced within a month of each round of competition.
Awards★	Individual and team awards vary, but include Mandelbrot playing cards.

Competition★	**Manningham Student Poetry Awards**
Sponsor★	National Federation of State Poetry Societies 501 Amsden Denison, TX 75021
Web Address★	http://www.nfsps.com/student_awards.htm
Area★	Language arts
Competition Origin★	1959
Purpose★	To encourage and support the writing of poetry.
Description★	Students can submit poems of any form on any subject and up to 50 lines. A contest brochure can be sent if a self-addressed, stamped envelope is mailed to the sponsor. Guidelines are also available online.
Eligibility★	Students in grades 6–12. There are two grade divisions: Junior (6–8) and Senior (9–12).
Important Dates★	The deadline for entry is mid-March. See guidelines for specific dates.
How to Enter★	Send a poem (limit one per student) to the state coordinator for submission. Coordinators' contact details are located on the Web site.
Judging Criteria★	Must be an original poem.
Judges★	Judged anonymously by a poet who is a member of NFSPS with expertise in judging and chosen from prizewinners in other annual contests.
Winner Notification★	Winners are notified in early May.
Awards★	First prize: $75; second prize: $50; third prize: $40; fourth prize: $35; and five honorable mentions: $10 each. Winning poems are published in an anthology.
Advice★	Use correct grammar, fresh images, an interesting title, and some real content in your poem.

Competition★	**The Marie Walsh Sharpe Art Foundation Summer Seminar**
Sponsor★	The Marie Walsh Sharpe Art Foundation 711 N. Tejon, Ste. 120 Colorado Springs, CO 80903
Web Address★	http://www.sharpeartfdn.org
Area★	Visual arts
Competition Origin★	1987
Purpose★	To offer an intensive visual art studio program for high school juniors.
Description★	Students submit an application form with 6–10 copies of at least four individual works, two of which must be drawings; a written statement expressing the most memorable experience of his or her life; and a recommendation from a high school art teacher. All details are located on the Web site or can be obtained by writing to the sponsor after January. Brochures are mailed to all public and private schools in January.
Eligibility★	Students in grade 11.
Important Dates★	Application deadline is in April. See guidelines for specific dates.
How to Enter★	Contact the sponsor or download the application from the Web site.
Judging Criteria★	The quality and originality of the work represented in the slides of the drawings is the primary criteria for receiving a scholarship. In the final round of deliberations, the recommendation and written statement is reviewed for the remaining applicants.
Judges★	A panel of jurors designated by the foundation select the participants for the summer seminar.
Winner Notification★	Winners are notified in late May.
Awards★	Full-tuition awards including tuition, room, board, and all seminar-related expenses are provided. Transportation is not included.

★ ★

Advice★

Students need a recommendation from an art teacher, summarizing (a) their creative potential for original work, (b) how they interact with others, and (c) any other factors including aspects of character, personality, and health that bear on the applicant's ability to participate in the summer seminar program.

Competition★	**MATHCOUNTS**
Sponsor★	MATHCOUNTS Foundation 1420 King St. Alexandria, VA 22314
Web Address★	http://mathcounts.org
Area★	Mathematics
Competition Origin★	1983
Purpose★	To promote student math achievement.
Description★	MATHCOUNTS is a national math coaching and competition program that promotes math achievement through grass-roots involvement in every U.S. state and territory. Guidelines may be obtained on the Web site or by writing to the sponsor.
Eligibility★	Students in grades 6–8.
Important Dates★	Kits are distributed to schools in September. The registration deadline is in December. See guidelines for specific dates.
How to Enter★	School completes and forwards application to the sponsor.
Judging Criteria★	Vary with math-related area of competition.
Judges★	Professionals in mathematics and related areas.
Winner Notification★	Winners are announced at each level of competition.
Awards★	Individual and team awards at regional and national levels vary.

Competition★	**Mathematical Olympiads for Elementary and Middle Schools**
Sponsor★	Mathematical Olympiads for Elementary and Middle Schools 2154 Bellmore Ave. Bellmore, NY 11710-5645
Web Address★	http://www.moems.org
Area★	Mathematics
Competition Origin★	1979
Purpose★	To stimulate enthusiasm and a love for mathematics.
Description★	Five contests (Olympiads) are administered during the school year, given from November to March. Guidelines may be obtained online.
Eligibility★	Students in grades 4–8.
Important Dates★	Enrollments are due by the end of September. See guidelines for specific dates.
How to Enter★	Write for registration form and other information, or have your school enroll online.
Judging Criteria★	Each Olympiad contains five open-ended questions with a time limit on each. If a student gets a correct answer, he or she receives a point and his or her team is credited with one point.
Judges★	Accuracy of answers.
Awards★	Each participant receives a certificate of participation. The high scorer of each team receives a trophy. Other awards include Olympiad patches, pins, medallions, and plaques.
Winner Notification★	Winners are notified in April.
Advice★	There are costs associated with this competition, so talk to your mathematics teacher to get started. The Web site also contains sample problems and lots of important information.

Competition★	**Medusa Mythology Exam**
Sponsor★	Medusa Mythology Examination P.O. Box 1032 Gainesville, VA 20156
Web Address★	http://www.medusaexam.org
Area★	Classical literature/mythology
Competition Origin★	1995
Purpose★	The Medusa was developed in order to allow those talented in mythology an opportunity to excel and be recognized. Another aim is to increase students' exposure to mythology.
Description★	The Medusa is composed of 50 multiple choice questions. The 2005 theme was "Oracles & Prophecies." Sources included the ancient works of Apollodorus, Homer, Ovid, and Virgil, and modern works such as Hamilton's *Mythology*, Bulfinch's *Age of Fable*, and Pierre Grimal's *Dictionary of Classical Mythology*. In the fall, a flyer, registration form, and syllabus will automatically be mailed to those schools where students have participated in the past. If you would like to have your school added to the mailing list, please contact the Medusa Exam Committee. You may also download the registration materials from the Web site.
Eligibility★	Students in grades 9–12.
Important Dates★	The exam is administered in early April each year. See guidelines for specific dates.
How to Enter★	Register online or via mail.
Judging Criteria★	Accuracy of answers.
Judges★	The Medusa Exam Committee, a team of 10 professors, teachers, and students, design the syllabus and questions for the exam. In addition, a panel of esteemed teachers reviews the initial copy of the exam to ensure its complete mythological accuracy. The Medusa Exam Committee then reviews the final copy of the exam.
Winner Notification★	Winners are notified in May.

Awards★

Top achievers on the exam receive certificates or medals imported from Italy. Highest-scoring participants are able to apply for several Achievement Awards to assist with educational expenses.

Advice★

Past exams can be downloaded from the Web site. There is a small fee for participation, but financial aid is available.

Competition★	**Modern Woodmen of America School Speech Contest**
Sponsor★	Modern Woodmen of America Attn: Fraternal Department Youth Division 1701 1st Ave., P.O. Box 2005 Rock Island, IL 61204-2005
Web Address★	http://www.modern-woodmen.org
Area★	Language arts
Competition Origin★	1948
Purpose★	To give students an opportunity to gain new public speaking skills, fine-tune existing English skills, and enhance self-esteem.
Description★	Each school year there is a new topic. Students get 3–5 minutes to discuss that topic. Topics usually come from suggestions by teachers who use the program. Guidelines and applications are available on the Web site or by contacting your local Modern Woodmen representative.
Eligibility★	Students in grades 5–12, but with a focus on grades 5–8. At national level, the competition is only for students in grades 5–8.
Important Dates★	Arranged by local schools. Contests can be held anytime from January through May.
How to Enter★	Contact your local Modern Woodmen representative to arrange for a speech contest in your school.
Judging Criteria★	Speeches are judged on material organization; delivery and presentation; and overall effectiveness.
Judges★	Appointed by local school for first level of competition and by the sponsor for regional and national levels.
Winner Notification★	Winners of competitions are recognized on-site.
Awards★	The winners of each school's Speech Contest can advance to the higher levels. At the national level, contestants compete for $1,250; $1,000; and $750 savings plans. (The savings plans, plus interest, will be paid to the winners when they become of legal age.)
Advice★	The contest may not be available in parts of the country.

★ ★

Competition★	**NASA Student Involvement Program (NSIP)**
Sponsor★	Office of Education Code N NASA Headquarters Washington, D.C. 20546-0001
Web Address★	http://www.nisp.net
Area★	Science
Competition Origin★	1980
Purpose★	To encourage students to become involved in the hands-on educational experience of space science competitions.
Description★	The NASA Student Involvement Program (NSIP) is a national program of six competitions linking students in grades K–12 directly with NASA's diverse and exciting mission of exploration, research, and discovery. Students may prepare entries as individuals, as teams of two to four, or as a whole class, depending on the competition category and grade level. Guidelines may be obtained on the Web site or by writing to the sponsor.
Eligibility★	Students in grades K–12.
Important Dates★	Contact sponsor for information on each competition, as dates vary.
How to Enter★	Information on each year's competitions, entry checklists, application forms, and details of upcoming events is available on the NSIP Web site. Each NSIP competition category has a Resource Guide for teachers that provides instructional materials, tips, and resources for using investigations and design challenges.
Judging Criteria★	Vary with each competition.
Judges★	Selected by NSTA and NASA.
Winner Notification★	Varies with each competition.
Awards★	Students and teachers can win trips to various NASA centers, internships with NASA scientists, space camp scholarships, medals, ribbons, certificates, and national recognition.
Advice★	Talk to your teacher about enrolling in these competitions.

115

Competition★	**National Current Events League**
Sponsor★	National Current Events League Box 2196 St. James, NY 11780-0605
Web Address★	http://www.continentalmathleague.hostrack.com/ Natcur.htm
Area★	Social studies
Competition Origin★	1993
Purpose★	To improve knowledge of current events.
Description★	Meets are held four times a year in your local school, and each meet consists of 30 multiple-choice questions. Guidelines may be obtained on the Web site or by writing to the sponsor.
Eligibility★	Students in grades 4–12.
Important Dates★	Schools need to register by mid-October. See guidelines for specific dates.
How to Enter★	Register by mail to the sponsor. The application can be downloaded from the Web site.
Judging Criteria★	Each test is proctored and scored by the school using the scoring sheet provided.
Judges★	Accuracy of answers.
Winner Notification★	Winners are notified in April.
Awards★	Medals and certificates are given to winners.
Advice★	Costs are involved for each team registration, so talk to your teacher or principal.

Competition★	**National Federation of Music Clubs Competitions**
Sponsor★	National Federation of Music Clubs 1336 North Delaware St. Indianapolis, IN 46202-2481
Web Address★	http://www.nfmc-music.org
Area★	Performing arts
Competition Origin★	1898
Purpose★	To develop and enhance student skills in music.
Description★	Scholarships and awards in music are granted through a variety of student competitions. More information and the guidelines are available on the Web site.
Eligibility★	Students ages 16–25. There are two divisions: Junior Age (must not have reached their 19th birthday by March 1) and Student Age (must have reached 16th but not 26th birthday by March 1). Entrants ages 16–18 may enter either Junior or Student competitions, but not both at the same time.
Important Dates★	Varies with the competitions. See guidelines for specific dates.
How to Enter★	Write to sponsor for scholarship and awards chart or browse the Web site.
Judging Criteria★	Exemplifies excellence in area of competition.
Judges★	Music professionals.
Winner Notification★	Varies with the competitions.
Awards★	More than $750,000 competition and award prizes are awarded on the local, state, and national level.

Competition★	**National Federation of Press Women High School Communications Contest**
Sponsor★	National Federation of Press Women P.O. Box 5556 Arlington, VA 22205
Web Address★	http://www.nfpw.org
Area★	Journalism
Competition Origin★	1998
Purpose★	To recognize excellent journalistic work and to inspire students to do their best work, which earns them recognition and reflects well on their teachers/advisers.
Description★	In the contest, students may enter work in one of 12 categories: Editorial, Opinion, News, Feature, Sports, Column, Feature Photo, Sports Photo, Cartooning, Reviews, Graphics and Single-Page Layout. Guidelines may be obtained on the Web site or by writing to the sponsor.
Eligibility★	Students in grades 9–12.
Important Dates★	Each state determines its deadline to allow time for judging and processing for the national contest so inquire early in the school year. The work must have been completed during the current year. See guidelines for specific dates.
How to Enter★	Contact state affiliate or visit the Web site.
Judging Criteria★	See the contest guidelines for specific judging criteria for each contest.
Judges★	National Federation of Press Women officials at state and national levels.
Winner Notification★	Winners are announced at an awards luncheon held at each year's national conference.
Awards★	Awards in each category include: $100 cash for first place; plaques for second and third places; and certificates for honorable mentions. National student winners, their parents, and advisers are invited to attend the NFPW Youth Projects Awards luncheon, which is held during the annual conference in September. Some affiliates provide financial assistance to students who attend the conference to accept their awards.

Advice★

Those residing in a state with no National Federation of Press Women affiliate may compete nationally on an at-large basis.

Competition★	*National Geographic* Bee
Sponsor★	National Geographic Society 1145 17th St. N.W. Washington, DC 20036-4688
Web Address★	http://www.nationalgeographic.com/geographybee
Area★	Social studies
Competition Origin★	1989
Purpose★	To encourage the teaching and study of geography.
Description★	Principals of schools must register and each school conducts the first competition, consisting of both oral and written elements. The student winners progress through the qualifying test, state, and national level competitions. Write to the National Geographic Society for details or visit the Web site.
Eligibility★	Students in grades 4–8.
Important Dates★	School competitions are held in mid-November through mid-January. State competitions are held in early spring. National competitions are held in late May. See guidelines for specific dates.
How to Enter★	Principals must register their schools before the October deadline to participate in the program. The application form is available online.
Judging Criteria★	Based on correctness and completeness of answers to oral and written questions concerning geography.
Judges★	At the school and qualifying test levels, a school representative is the judge. A state bee coordinator administrates at the state level, and the National Geographic Society administrates the national competition.
Winner Notification★	Winners are announced on the date of competition.
Awards★	The national first-place winner receives a $25,000 college scholarship; second place receives a $15,000 college scholarship; and third place receives a $10,000 college scholarship.
Advice★	There are some helpful study materials available on the Web site. The school must pay a fee to receive the contest materials, and at least six eligible students must compete.

Competition★	**National Geography Challenge**
Sponsor★	National Council for Geographic Education (NCGE) National Geography Challenge P.O. Box 2196 St. James, NY 11780-0605
Web Address★	http://www.ncge.org/activities/challenge.html
Area★	Social studies
Competition Origin★	1986
Purpose★	To improve geography skills.
Description★	A multiple-choice test is administered to students in April at their local school. The challenges reflect age-appropriate themes in geography. Guidelines may be obtained on the Web site or by writing to the sponsor.
Eligibility★	Students in grades 2–12. There are five grade divisions: 2; 3–4; 5–6; 7–9; and 10–12.
Important Dates★	The National Geography Challenge is held in April. Schools should register by mid-October. See guidelines for specific dates.
How to Enter★	Register by mail to the sponsor. An application is available on the Web site.
Judging Criteria★	Accuracy of answers.
Judges★	School officials use the sponsor's scoring key. National results are tabulated by the sponsor.
Winner Notification★	Winners are notified in May.
Awards★	Medals and certificates are given to the winners at each school. National awards are given for individuals and schools.
Advice★	Each team must pay registration fees, so talk to your principal or teacher to get your school signed up.

Competition★	**National High School Oratorical Competition**
Sponsor★	The American Legion National Headquarters P.O. Box 1055 Indianapolis, IN 46206-1055
Web Address★	http://www.legion.org
Areas★	Language arts and social studies
Competition Origin★	1938
Purpose★	To develop a deeper knowledge and appreciation of the Constitution of the United States. Other objectives include leadership, the ability to think and speak clearly and intelligently, and the preparation for the acceptance of the duties and responsibilities, as well as the rights and privileges of American citizenship.
Description★	Prepared orations must be based upon the Constitution of the United States. Assigned topics, which follow the prepared orations, are also based on the Constitution. All contestants speak on the same assigned topics. Prepared orations must be 8–10 minutes in length, with the assigned topics running from 3–5 minutes. Guidelines may be obtained on the Web site or by writing to the sponsor.
Eligibility★	Students in grades 9–12.
Important Dates★	Department (state) contests are usually held during the month of March. Dates for the National Regionals and Sectionals and the National Finals Contest are determined by The American Legion National Americanism Commission and are published in the annual Oratorical Contest Rules brochure. These contests are usually held during the month of April.
How to Enter★	Contact your local, state, or National American Legion Headquarters (The Americanism and Children and Youth Division).
Judging Criteria★	Contact the sponsor for information on judging criteria.
Judges★	Each contest uses five judges. Judges are typically from the legal profession, educators, the media, and the clergy.

Winner Notification★ Winners are announced at each level of competition.

Awards★ A National Scholarship fund of more than $100,000 is provided by The American Legion Life Insurance Committee and divided among regional and national winners. National winners receive: first place, $18,000; second place, $16,000; and third place, $14,000.

Advice★ The National Organization of The American Legion will pay the travel cost of department winners and their chaperones as they progress in the national competition. All contestants must be accompanied by a chaperone.

Competition★	**National History Day Contest**
Sponsor★	National History Day, Inc. 0119 Cecil Hall University of Maryland College Park, MD 20742
Web Address★	http://nationalhistoryday.org/02_contest/02.html
Area★	Social studies
Competition Origin★	1974
Purpose★	To encourage the study of social studies by guiding students to express themselves creatively through presentations of historical topics in various formats.
Description★	National History Day is a year-long educational program that fosters academic achievement and intellectual growth in secondary school students. By participating in a series of district, state, and national competitions, students develop research and reading skills, refine presentation and performance skills, and develop critical thinking and problem-solving skills that will help them manage and use information effectively now and in the future. Guidelines are available on the Web site.
Eligibility★	Students in grades 6–12. There are two grade divisions: Junior Division (6–8) and Senior Division (9–12).
Important Dates★	Contact your state sponsor in late summer or early fall for details. They are listed on the Web site.
How to Enter★	Contact your state sponsor.
Judging Criteria★	Varies with area of competition.
Judges★	Professionals such as educators and historians.
Winner Notification★	Winners are announced at the contest.
Awards★	At each level of competition, outstanding achievement may be recognized through certificates, medals, trophies, monetary awards, scholarships, or special prizes that may vary from year to year.
Advice★	Successful History Day entries include not only a description of the topic, but analysis and interpretation. It is important to place your topic into historical context and perspective. Ask yourself the follow-

ing questions about your topic: Why is my topic important? How was my topic significant in history in relation to the History Day theme? How did my topic develop over time? How did my topic influence history? How did the events and atmosphere (social, economic, political, and cultural aspects) of my topic's time period influence my topic in history?

Competition★	The National Latin Exam
Sponsor★	National Latin Exam Mary Washington College 1301 College Ave. Fredericksburg, VA 22401
Web Address★	http://www.nle.org
Area★	Foreign language
Competition Origin★	1978
Purpose★	To promote an in-depth understanding of Latin.
Description★	Each exam is 40 minutes long and consists of 40 multiple-choice questions. Each exam tests students in the understanding of Latin grammar, comprehension, mythology, life, history, derivatives, and passages. Guidelines are listed on the Web site.
Eligibility★	Students enrolled in Latin or who have completed a course during the academic school year.
Important Dates★	The Latin exams are given during the second full week in March. The exam must be mailed by mid-March. See guidelines for specific dates.
How to Enter★	An application form can downloaded through the National Latin Exam Web site. A registration fee from $4 to $6 is also required of students.
Judging Criteria★	The exams are graded for grammar, comprehension, content, and historical accuracy.
Judges★	Exams are scored by software.
Winner Notification★	Results are mailed out in April of each year.
Awards★	Certificates, medals, ribbons, and $1,000 scholarships are given.
Advice★	The Web site has a set of helpful FAQs (Frequently Asked Questions).

Competition★	**National Leadership Award and I Dare You Scholarship**
Sponsor★	American Youth Foundation 8706 Manchester Rd., Ste. 102 St. Louis, MO 63144
Web Address★	http://www.ayf.com/prog_idy_main.asp
Area★	Leadership
Competition Origin★	1941
Purpose★	To recognize the leadership capacity of high school students and 4-H participants.
Description★	Students are nominated for the National Leadership Award. Recipients of the awards are eligible for a I Dare You Scholarship, which provides funds toward tuition for the AYF Leadership Conference. The program is intended to focus on "emerging" leaders—those young adults who have the qualities and abilities to lead, but who may not yet recognize or have acted on their leadership potential. An application form is available on the Web site or can be requested in writing from the sponsor.
Eligibility★	Students ages 15–18.
Important Dates★	Contact the sponsor for details.
How to Enter★	Complete the selection form provided by sponsor.
Judging Criteria★	Recognition by peers and adults who work with students serving as emerging leaders.
Judges★	American Youth Foundation officials.
Winner Notification★	Winners are notified by the beginning of June.
Awards★	The National Leadership Award consists of three elements: a personalized award certificate, a copy of *I Dare You!*, and eligibility to apply for a scholarship to the International Leadership Conferences.
Advice★	Scholarships awarded on a first-come, first-serve basis.

Competition★	**National Middle School Healthy Heritage Recipe Contest**
Sponsor★	Johnson and Wales University 8 Abbott Park Place Providence, RI 02903
Web Address★	http://www.healthykidschallenge.com/recipes.php
Area★	Culinary arts
Competition Origin★	2002
Purpose★	To allow the young chefs of tomorrow to showcase their culinary creativity, while also promoting healthy eating habits and nutritionally well-balanced food preparation with a focus on heritage.
Description★	Contestants can enter one recipe in one of the following categories: Healthy Heritage Snack, Healthy Heritage Salad/Appetizer, and Healthy Heritage Main Dish. Guidelines are on the Web site. They are also sent to Family and Consumer Science classes throughout the United States.
Eligibility★	Students in grades 7–8.
Important Dates★	Entries must be postmarked by late March. See guidelines for specific dates.
How to Enter★	Contact sponsor or talk to your teacher about an application. One can also be downloaded from the Web site.
Judging Criteria★	All recipes are judged on the following: nutritional value; relation to culture(s) reflected in description; originality and creativity; and presentation and appearance.
Judges★	A panel of judges selected by the sponsor selects recipe finalists.
Winner Notification★	Winners are notified in mid-April.
Awards★	Tons of cool prizes, plus $12,000 in tuition scholarships to Johnson and Wales University and "A Chef For A Day" on-site visit to your school during which time a Chef/Instructor from Johnson and Wales University will help demonstrate how to prepare the winning recipe.

Advice★

Don't forget to submit a color photograph of one prepared serving of your recipe.

Competition★	**National Mythology Exam**
Sponsor★	Excellence Through Classics American Classical League Miami University Oxford, OH 45056-1694
Web Address★	http://www.etclassics.org/myth_exam.htm
Area★	Classical literature/mythology
Competition Origin★	1989
Purpose★	To acquaint students with mythology and classical literature, including African and Native American myths.
Description★	Students take a multiple-choice exam on mythology and classical literature. Guidelines may be obtained on the Web site or by writing to the sponsor.
Eligibility★	Students in grades 3–9.
Important Dates★	Registration is by mid-January. Administration of exam is usually in late February or early March. See guidelines for specific dates.
How to Enter★	Contact sponsor in writing or enter online.
Judging Criteria★	Accuracy of answers.
Judges★	Exams are scored by machines.
Winner Notification★	Winners are notified in late April.
Awards★	Prizes include certificates of excellence and bronze medallions.
Advice★	The Web site has sample questions and study guidelines available online.

Competition★	**National Peace Essay Contest**
Sponsor★	United States Institute of Peace 1200 17th St. NW Washington, DC 20036
Web Address★	http://www.usip.org/ed/npec
Areas★	Language arts and social studies
Competition Origin★	1996
Purpose★	To promote serious discussion among high school students, teachers, and national leaders about international peace and conflict resolution; complement existing curricula; and strengthen students' research, writing, and reasoning skills.
Description★	Students write an essay on the chosen theme, which may focus on topics such as international affairs, conflict resolution, social studies, history, or politics. The competition guidelines and application forms are available on the Web site.
Eligibility★	Students in grades 9–12.
Important Dates★	The deadline for entry is early February. See guidelines for specific dates.
How to Enter★	Students submit a 1,500 word essay on the chosen topic. Three copies are sent to the sponsor with an application form.
Judging Criteria★	Each aspect of the given topic must be addressed. Entries are judged for their research, analysis, and form.
Judges★	Essays are sent to state-level judges who are appointed by the Institute.
Winner Notification★	Winners are notified in May.
Awards★	First-place state winners receive college scholarships of $1,000. First-place state winners also compete for national awards of $10,000, $5,000, and $2,500 for first, second, and third place respectively (national awards include state award amounts). All first place state winners are invited to attend an all-expenses-paid awards program in Washington, DC, in June.

Competition★	**National Portuguese Exam**
Sponsor★	American Association of Teachers of Spanish and Portuguese (AATSP) 423 Exton Commons Exton, PA 19341-2451
Web Address★	https://www.aatsp.org
Area★	Foreign language
Competition Origin★	2003
Purpose★	To test student language skills in Portuguese.
Description★	Students taking the exams are grouped into levels, depending on their in-class and out-of-class experience with Portuguese. Highest scorers in each level are recognized at the chapter (state) level and national level. Tests are administered at the school setting. Any Portuguese teacher who is an AATSP member in good standing may enter students in the competition. Guidelines may be obtained on the Web site or by writing to the sponsor.
Eligibility★	Students of Portuguese in grades K–12. The teacher must be a member of AATSP.
Important Dates★	Testing takes place between mid-February and mid-March. See guidelines for specific dates.
How to Enter★	Teachers need to register their classes by contacting the AATSP.
Judging Criteria★	Accuracy of answers.
Judges★	Teacher-scored.
Winner Notification★	Winners are notified upon completion and scoring of examination.
Awards★	Recognition will vary within each school. Students who participate are ranked on the local and national levels based on results.

Competition★	**National Social Studies League**
Sponsor★	National Social Studies League P.O. Box 2196 St. James, NY 11780-0605
Web Address★	http://www.continentalmathleague.hostrack.com/Natsoc.htm
Area★	Social studies
Competition Origin★	1993
Purpose★	To improve social studies skills.
Description★	A multiple-choice test on social studies is administered to participating students. These questions are based on topics in American Studies, geography of the United States, and United States government, appropriate to each grade level. Guidelines may be obtained on the Web site or by writing to the sponsor.
Eligibility★	Students in grades 2–12.
Important Dates★	The deadline for registration is mid-October. See guidelines for specific dates.
How to Enter★	Register by mailing an application to the sponsor. The application can be downloaded from the Web site.
Judging Criteria★	Accuracy of answers.
Judges★	Local school officials use sponsor's scoring key. Sponsor tabulates national results.
Winner Notification★	Winners are notified in May.
Awards★	Medals and certificates to local winners. National winners are also recognized with individual and team awards.
Advice★	There are registration fees required for each school's team, so talk to your teacher or principal.

Competition★	**National Society Daughters of the American Revolution Good Citizens Contest**
Sponsor★	National Society Daughters of the American Revolution 1776 D St. N.W. Washington, DC 20006
Web Address★	http://www.dar.org
Area★	Social studies
Competition Origin★	1934
Purpose★	To encourage and reward the qualities of good citizenship.
Description★	The DAR Good Citizens Scholarship Contest consists of two parts. Part I (personal) is a series of questions asking the student to describe how he or she has tried to manifest the qualities of a good citizen. This part may be completed at home and is to be submitted together with a copy of his or her scholastic record and one letter of recommendation. Part II (essay) is to be administered under the supervision of a faculty or DAR member. It must be completed at one sitting, within a 2-hour time limit, and without assistance or reference materials. Information can be obtained through the DAR chairman in your state.
Eligibility★	Students in grade 12.
Important Dates★	State first-place division winner entries should be sent to national chair by mid-February. See guidelines for specific dates.
How to Enter★	Contact the DAR Good Citizen chair of the state in which you live.
Judging Criteria★	Must have qualities of dependability, service, leadership, and patriotism.
Judges★	The State Society DAR and the State Department of Education determine the method of selection of the State DAR Good Citizen. Each school chooses its own student as the School DAR Good Citizen.
Winner Notification★	Winners are notified in March.

Awards★

The national awards are as follows: The first-place winner receives a $5,000 scholarship; the second-place winner receives $2,000; and the third-place winner receives $1,000. Each state and division winner receives $250.

Advice★

Each chapter chairman should obtain the cooperation of the school administration as soon as possible so that the DAR Good Citizen program contest may be included in the schedule.

Competition★	**National Spanish Exam**
Sponsors★	The American Association of Teachers of Spanish and Portuguese 423 Exton Commons Exton, PA 19341-2451
Web Address★	http://www.2nse.org
Area★	Foreign language
Competition Origin★	1957
Purpose★	To motivate students to learn more about the Spanish language and culture.
Description★	Students are given a test with questions on Spanish vocabulary and grammar. Information for the exams may be found on the Web site or by contacting the sponsor.
Eligibility★	Students in grades 11–12 who are enrolled in a Spanish class.
Important Dates★	Exams are given between mid-February and mid-March. See guidelines for specific dates.
How to Enter★	Teachers must enter the students. This may be done through the Web site or by contacting the sponsor.
Judging Criteria★	Accuracy of answers.
Judges★	Exams are scored by computer.
Winner Notification★	Names of national winners are published in the September issue of the AATSP journal.
Awards★	The students with the top five scores at the national level are awarded plaques.
Advice★	There are various study materials available on the Web site.

Competition★	**National Women's Hall of Fame Essay and New Media Contest**
Sponsor★	National Women's Hall of Fame 76 Fall Street, P.O. Box 335 Seneca Falls, NY 13148
Web Address★	http://www.greatwomen.org
Areas★	Language arts and technology
Competition Origin★	1982
Purpose★	To honor women whose contributions to American society have been of great value to our country.
Description★	Entrants are asked to create a Web page or electronic presentation. Entries in each category must explore the work of a Hall Inductee and demonstrate how that woman's achievement changed the world we live in today. Each year a theme is selected; for example, in 2004 the theme was "Women as Changemakers." Guidelines may be obtained on the Web site or by writing to the sponsor.
Eligibility★	Students in grades 4–12. The Essay Contest is open to students grades 4–12. The New Media Contest is open to students in grades 6–12.
Important Dates★	Deadline for entry is mid-April. See guidelines for specific dates.
How to Enter★	Write for guidelines or visit the Web site.
Judging Criteria★	Essays are judged within grade groups on creativity, historical accuracy, spelling and grammar mechanics, and organization. The scoring criteria for New Media focus on originality, design, historical accuracy, and readability.
Judges★	Entries are judged by members of Delta Kappa Gamma Society International.
Winner Notification★	Winners are notified in May.
Awards★	The top three entrants in each category of the New Media and Essay divisions receive a certificate of achievement and cash prizes.

Competition★	**National Young Astronomer Award**
Sponsor★	The Astronomical League National Office Manager 9201 Ward Parkway Ste. #100 Kansas City, MO 64114
Web Address★	http://www.astroleague.org/al/awards/nyaa/ noya.html
Area★	Science
Competition Origin★	1993
Purpose★	To recognize outstanding achievement in astronomy by amateur astronomers.
Description★	A national panel of judges selects the winner based upon the student's overall achievements in astronomy. Activities that the judges consider include astronomical research, astronomical articles published, local astronomical club activities, academic achievements in science and math, involvement in regional and national astronomy organizations, observing history and skills, astrophotography and/or CCD Imaging, public education experience, and telescope design. Guidelines may be obtained on the Web site or by writing to the sponsor.
Eligibility★	Students in grades 9–12 or who are 14 to 19 years of age and not enrolled in college on the application deadline.
Important Dates★	The deadline for submission is late January. See guidelines for specific dates.
How to Enter★	Complete the application form and obtain a sponsor's signature. Prepare a typewritten summary of your achievements in astronomy, enclosing optional exhibits. Mail the application form, summary, and exhibits to the award chairperson by the award deadline.
Judging Criteria★	Award selections are, by their very nature, subjective. Accordingly, the league warrants only that awards will be presented to individuals who, in the opinion of the national judges, merit the awards. Because of staffing constraints and difficulties inherent in the award process, the award chairperson may extend deadlines or respond to special needs and circum-

stances in administering the award. Judges' rankings are averaged using Zip's Law (e.g., third place vote equals ⅓ point, fourth place vote equals ¼ point). Ties are broken by the lowest total of raw rankings.

Judges★

The NOYAA committee selects a national panel of judges consisting of well-known amateur and professional astronomers who review all application packages and select 10 finalists. Currently, all judges are professional physicists and astronomers.

Winner Notification★

Winners are notified in mid-March.

Awards★

The first-place winner receives a Meade 10 inch LX-200 Schmidt-Cassegrain Telescope valued at about $3,000. The winner also receives an all-expenses-paid trip to the League's national convention to receive the award. The University of Texas McDonald Observatory presents "lifetime passes" to the first and second place winners. Plaques are presented to the first-, second-, and third-place winners at the League's national convention each summer.

Competition★	*NewsCurrents* **Student Editorial Cartoon Contest**
Sponsor★	NewsCurrents Cartoon Contest. P.O. Box 52 Madison, WI 53701
Web Address★	http://www.newscurrents.com/intro/edcartoons/carcon2.html
Areas★	Journalism and visual arts
Competition Origin★	1989
Purpose★	To showcase the complex thinking and communications skills young people are capable of when challenged with effective curricular materials.
Description★	Entrants must submit original cartoons on any subject of national or international interest. Each entry must include the following information written on the back of the cartoon: student's name, grade, school, school address, school phone number, and the signature of a teacher verifying that the cartoon is the original work of the student. Guidelines are available on the Web site.
Eligibility★	Students in grades K–12. There are three grade divisions: K–6, 7–9, and 10–12.
Important Dates★	Entries must be postmarked by the beginning of March. See guidelines for specific dates.
How to Enter★	Mail entries to the sponsor's address.
Judging Criteria★	Entries are judged primarily on the basis of originality, clarity of idea, and knowledge of subject. Artistic quality is considered secondarily.
Judges★	The judges consist of the editorial staff of *NewsCurrents*.
Winner Notification★	Winners will be notified by mid-April.
Awards★	First-, second-, and third-place winners are chosen from each grade category. Winners receive U.S. savings bonds. The top two winners are published in an issue of the weekly *NewsCurrents Current Events* program, viewed by more than one million students. One hundred of the best entries are also be selected to be published in a book by Knowledge Unlimited titled *Editorial Cartoons By Kids*. Students whose cartoons are selected for the book receive a free copy.

★ ★

Advice★

Judges recommend that cartoons be drawn with black ink on white paper. Use bold lines and make letters large enough to be read easily. Draw the cartoons in a horizontal format. Don't create a cartoon that is nothing more than a simple slogan or a poster. Be thought provoking and original. Entries sent after the deadline will automatically be entered in the next year's contest.

Competition★	**Odyssey of the Mind Program**
Sponsor★	Odyssey of the Mind Program c/o Creative Competitions, Inc. 1325 Rt. 130 South, Ste. F Gloucester City, NJ 08030
Web Address★	http://www.odysseyofthemind.com
Area★	Creativity/problem solving
Competition Origin★	1978
Purpose★	To foster creative thinking and provide creative problem-solving opportunities for all students.
Description★	Each team performs its solution within a specified time frame and within certain cost limits. OM charters affiliates that run the local and state (association finals) competitions. These competitions culminate with an International OM World Finals competition held annually in late May or early June. Competing teams in this event represent top finishers in each U. S. state and many international counties. Guidelines may be obtained on the Web site or by writing to the sponsor.
Eligibility★	Students in grades K–12 and college. There are four grade divisions: Division I (K–5); Division II (6–8); Division III (9–12); and Division IV (Collegiate).
Important Dates★	Local competitions begin in January and end with the OM World Finals in late May or early June. The OM membership year runs concurrent with the school year. See guidelines for specific dates.
How to Enter★	Each member is entitled to participate in the local competition. Registration varies from state to state. Contact your local association director.
Judging Criteria★	There is no right or wrong answer to any problem, but there are both limitations and a specific end result that must be achieved. Teams are judged in three areas. The first is in the "long-term" problem, that is, the solution that the team has created and showcases in the competition. The second is style or how one "markets" or elaborates the solution. This may be achieved by the use of such elements as music, dance, costumes, script, and so on. Finally, spontaneity area is judged as a third category. Each

team receives a problem to solve the day of the competition. The team must solve it on the spot without any preparation and within a time limit.

Judges★

Judges are adult volunteers trained before the competition. Some are educators, some are business people, and others are interested parents, supporters, and former team members.

Winner Notification★

Winners are announced at an awards ceremony following each competition.

Awards★

Awards vary, but are generally medals, trophies, and certificates.

Advice★

Purchase membership materials at the beginning of the school year. Local competitions begin as early as January, and students need time to develop, troubleshoot, and fine tune solutions.

Competition★	**Olympiada of Spoken Russian**
Sponsor★	American Councils of Teachers of Russian 1776 Massachusetts Ave., NW, Ste. 700 Washington, DC 20036
Web Address★	http://www.americancouncils.org
Area★	Foreign language
Competition Origin★	1962
Purpose★	This competition is for U.S. high school students to demonstrate excellence in Russian language.
Description★	This contest involves speaking about yourself, reading, and the civilization of Russia. Guidelines may be obtained on the Web site or by writing to the sponsor.
Eligibility★	Students in grades 9–12 who are winners of state and regional Olympiada contests.
Important Dates★	State competitions must be finalized by late April for participation at national level. See guidelines for specific dates.
How to Enter★	A teacher who is a member of ACTR must enter a student. This can be done through the Web site or by contacting the sponsor.
Judging Criteria★	Spoken fluency of Russian language.
Judges★	Teachers of Russian and members of ACTR.
Winner Notification★	State winners are notified for participation in national program.
Awards★	Medals and certificates are distributed at an awards ceremony held at the school for the winners. The top students in each region (gold medalists) are invited to take part in a summer immersion program in Russia sponsored by ACTR. In addition, every third year, an international Olympiada contest is convened in Moscow, during which students of Russian from around the world and winners of the Olympiadas in their respective countries gather in Moscow to compete for the international medals, as well as engage in a rich program of cultural activities, performances, and juries.

Advice★

Students need to be aware that there is a $1,000 program fee, plus cost of international and U.S. domestic airfare, for those going to Russia. The American Councils funds all other program costs.

Competition★	**Outstanding Young Volunteer of the Year**
Sponsor★	Ladies Auxiliary Veterans of Foreign Wars (VFW) 406 W. 34th St. Kansas City, MO 64111
Web Address★	http://www.ladiesauxvfw.com/outstand.html
Area★	Service learning
Competition Origin★	1991
Purpose★	To recognize outstanding volunteerism amongst youth.

Description★

Students send in an entry form and three letters of recommendation from the organization for which they volunteer to the Auxiliary Youth Activities Chairperson. Letter should be on letterhead stationery and should include the following:

- How well you perform the work;
- How your volunteer work affects others;
- How many hours you spend on each project; and
- The number of groups for which you volunteer.

The "Why I Am A Volunteer" section must be completed by the student and must include fewer than 150 words explaining how volunteer efforts go above and beyond normal activities. Contact your state Auxiliary or visit the Web site for more information.

Eligibility★

Students ages 12–15. Students must be sponsored by an Auxiliary.

Important Dates★

Student applications are due at the beginning of February. See guidelines for specific dates.

How to Enter★

Download an application form from the Web site.

Judging Criteria★

Judges consider the number of volunteer activities in which the applicant has been involved. Activities could include volunteering in hospitals and nursing homes, aiding senior citizens, assisting in Buddy Poppy campaigns, providing services to veterans, involvement in scouting, church or school programs, and other activities that serve the community. In addition, the quality of service will also be considered, such as an individual who has accomplished one truly outstanding achievement.

Judges★

Judges on all levels are community leaders and individuals who work with young people, such as teachers, church officials, scout leaders, YWCA staff, and so forth.

Winner Notification★

Winners are notified in advance of the national convention, which is held mid-year.

Awards★

The top National Winner will receive a $5,000 U.S. Savings Bond, a plaque, and airfare with two nights' lodging to attend the Ladies Auxiliary VFW National Convention.

Advice★

When submitting your application, do not send scrapbooks.

Competition★	The Panasonic Academic Challenge
Sponsor★	Panasonic Consumer Electronics Company P.O. 391 Bartow, FL 33831
Web Address★	http://www.polk-fl.net/ac/PAC.html
Area★	Academic quiz bowl
Competition Origin★	1988
Purpose★	To foster academic competition in a team setting.
Description★	The Panasonic Academic Challenge is a highly academic national high school competition. Each team consists of six students (four players and two alternates) and one coach. As many as six teams may compete against each other in one competition. This is not a quick response, trivial pursuit contest. Instead, it is a slower-paced tournament in which players are asked questions from the areas of mathematics, science, language arts, social studies, the fine arts, foreign language (French and Spanish) and technology. Guidelines may be obtained on the Web site or by writing to the sponsor.
Eligibility★	Students in grades 9–12.
Important Dates★	State competition dates vary, but registration for the national competition is in March. The national competition is held in June. See guidelines for specific dates.
How to Enter★	Write to the sponsor.
Judging Criteria★	Criteria for each state team vary. Rules for the national tournament are located on the Web site.
Judges★	Appointed by the sponsors each year.
Winner Notification★	Winners are announced at the national championship.
Awards★	Each member and head coach of the national championship team receives a $2,500 scholarship and a ring. The second-place team members and head coach each receive a $1,500 scholarship and a ring. The third-place team members and head coach each receive a $500 scholarship and a ring. Six students are selected from the Panasonic Academic Challenge's participants to form the All America

Academic Team, and each member receives a $1,000 scholarship and a medallion.

Advice★

Register early. There are substantial costs involved for each participating team.

Competition★	**Panasonic Young Soloists Award**
Sponsor★	VSA Panasonic Young Soloists Award 1300 Connecticut Avenue, NW, Ste. 700 Washington, DC 20036
Web Address★	http://www.vsarts.org
Area★	Performing arts
Competition Origin★	1991
Purpose★	To recognize exceptional young musicians with disabilities.
Description★	Applicants are required to complete an application form and submit a brief autobiography, as well as a videotape or audio cassette recording. Contact the sponsor for guidelines or download them from the Web site.
Eligibility★	Musically talented students, ages 25 and under, with a disability.
Important Dates★	Entries are due in early November. See guidelines for specific dates.
How to Enter★	Request an application packet from the sponsor or download it from the Web site.
Judging Criteria★	Technique, tone, intonation (if applicable), rhythm, and interpretation.
Judges★	Professional musicians and music educators.
Winner Notification★	Winners are notified in January.
Awards★	Soloists who earn scholarship funds are invited to perform at The John F. Kennedy Center for the Performing Arts.
Advice★	Students living outside the United States may be eligible for the Rosemary Kennedy International Young Soloists competition. Information on this competition is available on the Web site.

Competition★	**Patriot's Pen**
Sponsor★	Veterans of Foreign Wars of the United States VFW Building 406 W. 34th St. Kansas City, MO 06411
Web Address★	http://www.vfw.org
Areas★	Language arts and social studies
Competition Origin★	1995
Purpose★	To give students the opportunity to express their views on democracy.
Description★	Patriot's Pen is a nationwide competition that gives students the opportunity to write essays expressing their views on democracy. Contestants write a 300–400 word essay on a patriotic theme. Students advance from state competition to national competition. Visit the Web site for contest guidelines and contact information for the national headquarters or your local VFW Post.
Eligibility★	Students in grades 6–8.
Important Dates★	Entries are due at the beginning of November. See guidelines for specific dates.
How to Enter★	Contact the national headquarters or your local VFW Post. An entry form and rules can also be downloaded from the Web site.
Judging Criteria★	Knowledge of theme, theme development, and clarity of ideas.
Judges★	Appointed by the VFW.
Winner Notification★	Winners are notified in March.
Awards★	The first-place winner receives a $10,000 savings bond and an all-expenses-paid trip to Washington, DC. The top national winners each receive a savings bond anywhere from $1,000 to $10,000.
Advice★	Be sure to establish a contact with someone in your local VFW Post or Ladies Auxiliary.

Competition★	**Physics Bowl**
Sponsor★	American Association of Physics Teachers (AAPT) One Physics Ellipse College Park, MD 20740-3845
Web Address★	http://www.aapt.org/Contests/physicsbowl.cfm
Area★	Science
Competition Origin★	1994
Purpose★	To encourage interest in physics and recognize students' scientific achievement and excellence in teaching.
Description★	All students who enter take a 40-question, timed, multiple-choice test supervised at their school. Contest questions are based on topics and concepts in typical high school physics courses. Guidelines may be obtained on the Web site or by writing to the sponsor.
Eligibility★	Students in grades 9–12. There are two divisions: Division I (first year physics students) and Division II (second year physics students).
Important Dates★	Registration is in late March, with the testing during mid-April. See guidelines for specific dates.
How to Enter★	Request application materials via mail or online.
Judging Criteria★	Accuracy of answers.
Judges★	Tests are scored by machines.
Winner Notification★	Winners are notified as soon as individual and team scores are submitted and calculated by AAPT.
Awards★	All students and teachers who enter the Physics Bowl receive a certificate of participation from the AAPT. Sixty $100 gift certificates from Frey Scientific are awarded to teachers in the first- and second-place schools in each region. Sixty 1-year AAPT memberships awarded to teachers in the first- and second-place schools in each region. One TI-84 Plus Silver Edition calculator will be awarded by Texas Instruments to the top student in each region. An all-expenses-paid trip to the 2005 AAPT Summer Meeting is also awarded by Texas Instruments to the top student in each division. An all-expenses-paid trip to the Physics Teaching Resource Agents

Institute (PTRA) is awarded by Texas Instruments to the teacher from the top school in each division. T-shirts are awarded to the four top students in the top scoring school in each region.

★ ★

Competition★	**Pier 1/UNICEF/*Weekly Reader* Greeting Card Contest**
Sponsor★	Co-sponsored by UNICEF, Pier 1, and *Weekly Reader* United States Committee for UNICEF 333 E. 38th St. New York, NY 10016
Web Address★	http://www.unicefusa.org
Area★	Visual arts
Competition Origin★	1991
Purpose★	To allow children the opportunity to depict through artwork the ideal that even though kids can come from different countries, they all need the same things to survive and grow.
Description★	Children create greeting cards based upon a theme. Guidelines are available in April at Pier 1 stores and on the Web site (www.pier1.com).
Eligibility★	Students in grades K–6.
Important Dates★	Entries due in late April. See guidelines for specific dates.
How to Enter★	See official contest rules for details.
Judging Criteria★	Creativity and quality of expression.
Judges★	Officials from sponsoring organizations.
Winner Notification★	Winners are notified in early fall.
Awards★	Two grand prizes are awarded, one each in age group: 7 and under and 8–13. Each grand prize consists of a trip to a U.S. city selected by Pier 1 Imports, $500, and a 1-year *Weekly Reader* subscription. The two winning cards are printed by the U.S. Committee for UNICEF and sold exclusively at Pier 1 stores. Eight runners-up receive a 1-year *Weekly Reader* subscription, a donation to UNICEF made in their name, and a plaque.

Competition★	**Presidential Classroom Scholars Program**
Sponsor★	A Presidential Classroom for Young Americans, Inc. 119 Oronoco St. Alexandria, VA 22314-2015
Web Address★	http://www.presidentialclassroom.org
Areas★	Leadership and social studies
Competition Origin★	1968
Purpose★	To help prepare outstanding high school juniors and seniors for leadership and civic responsibility by providing firsthand exposure to the federal government in action.
Description★	This program allows leaders to be provided with strong academic and leadership development in Washington, DC. Guidelines may be obtained on the Web site or by writing to the sponsor.
Eligibility★	Students in grades 11–12 (rising juniors may attend summer sessions). Students must maintain at least a B average or rank in the top 25% of their class and submit the authorization of their school principal.
Important Dates★	Registration deadlines are in December and May. See guidelines for specific dates.
How to Enter★	Complete the application process.
Judging Criteria★	See eligibility requirements. Those interested in scholarship opportunities must demonstrate genuine financial need; maintain at least a 3.8 grade point average; and hold leadership positions in school or community organizations.
Judges★	Presidential Classroom staff.
Winner Notification★	Winners are notified upon receipt and acceptance of application.
Awards★	Limited scholarships available.

Competition★	**President's Environmental Youth Awards**
Sponsor★	U.S. Environmental Protection Agency 1200 Pennsylvania Ave., NW (1701A) Washington, DC 20460
Web Address★	http://www.epa.gov/enviroed/awards.html
Areas★	Science and service learning
Competition Origin★	1971
Purpose★	To offer young people an opportunity to become an environmental force within their community.
Description★	The program has two components: the regional certificate program and the national awards competition. Students are recognized for their efforts to make and keep the world around us a safer, cleaner place to live. Contact your regional EPA office for guidelines or look on the Web site.
Eligibility★	Students in grades K–12.
Important Dates★	Regional applications are accepted year-round; however, at the national level, applications must be submitted by the end of July. See guidelines for specific dates.
How to Enter★	Obtain an application and detailed guidelines from your regional EPA office or from the Web site.
Judging Criteria★	The judging panel considers the following: environmental need for the project; environmental appropriateness of the project, accomplishment of goals, long–term environmental benefits derived from the project; positive environmental impact on the local community and society; evidence of the young person's initiative, innovation, soundness of approach, rationale, and scientific design (if applicable); and clarity and effectiveness of presentation.
Judges★	Judging panel selected by the EPA.
Winner Notification★	Dates vary for regional contests. National winners are notified in the fall.
Awards★	All participants at the regional level receive certificates signed by the President of the United States honoring them for their efforts in environmental protection. The national winners, along with one project sponsor, receive an all-expenses-paid trip to

the National Awards Ceremony and consult with the EPA Youth Work Group about the program. They also receive a $1,000 grant from Keebler Company. Church & Dwight Company hosts a luncheon and presents an additional $1,000 grant to each winner, as well as a smaller grant to the three runners-up in each region.

Advice★

For winning ideas, have a look at the past winners' projects on the Web site.

Competition★	**PROJECT: Learn MS Scholarship Essay Competition**
Sponsor★	PROJECT: Learn MS 706 Haddonfield Road Cherry Hill, NJ 08002
Web Address★	http://www.parentsinc.org/finaid/aid6233.html
Area★	Language arts
Competition Origin★	1993
Purpose★	To provide students an opportunity to learn about the most prevalent neurological disease affecting young adults in the U.S. and to become aware of the special needs of the disabled community.
Description★	Students submit essays on the topic of multiple sclerosis. Guidelines may be obtained on the Web site or by writing to the sponsor.
Eligibility★	Students in grades 10–12 and college freshmen, sophomores, and juniors.
Important Dates★	Entries must be submitted by early June. See guidelines for specific dates.
How to Enter★	Write 500–1,000 words; collect sponsorship; complete registration form; and submit entry to sponsor.
Judging Criteria★	Originality, content, grammar, and style. Essays must address the following three topics:

1. What is multiple sclerosis?
2. How does it affect the family?
3. How do you feel that you personally and society as a whole can impact and improve daily living for people with disabilities?

Judges★	MSAA-selected judges.
Winner Notification★	Winners are notified by early summer.
Awards★	There are two $5,000 scholarships and six $1,000 scholarships given. Half of these awards are for high school students and half for those enrolled in college.
Advice★	With more than 1,300 entrants in 2004, it is important to submit your best piece of writing.

Competition★	**Promising Young Writers Program**
Sponsor★	National Council of Teachers of English 1111 W. Kenyon Road Urbana, IL 61801-1096
Web Address★	http://www.ncte.org/about/awards/student/pyw
Area★	Language arts
Competition Origin★	1984
Purpose★	To develop skills in writing.
Description★	Each participant must submit a "Best Writing Sample," which may be poetry or prose. They must also write on an "Impromptu Theme" developed by the Promising Young Writers Advisory Committee. Guidelines may be obtained on the Web site or by writing to the sponsor.
Eligibility★	Students in grade 8.
Important Dates★	Mid-January is the submission deadline. See guidelines for specific dates.
How to Enter★	Teachers complete a nomination form for each student nominee. This can be downloaded from the Web site or requested via mail.
Judging Criteria★	Papers are judged on content, purpose, audience, tone, word choice, organization, development, and style. Judges take into account that the writers are eighth grade students, not professional writers, and that the impromptu papers are written under time constraints.
Judges★	Teams of teachers at the state level will judge the writing.
Winner Notification★	All certificates are mailed to school principals, who are asked to present them to each student who submitted writing samples. Nominating teachers will also be notified.
Awards★	Each student who enters receives a citation. Certificates of recognition are awarded to students cited as winners. Certificates of participation are awarded to other nominees who write.
Advice★	There is an entry fee of $5 for this competition.

Competition★	**Prudential Spirit of Community Awards**
Sponsor★	Prudential Spirit of Community Awards One Scholarship Way P.O. Box 297 St. Peter, MN 56082
Web Address★	http://www.prudential.com/community/spirit
Areas★	Leadership and service learning
Competition Origin★	1995
Purpose★	To recognize students in middle and high school grades who have demonstrated exemplary community service.
Description★	Student applicants compete based upon a description of their community service project, highlighting their leadership role. Visit the Web site for guidelines.
Eligibility★	Students in grades 5–12 who have engaged in a volunteer activity in the 12 months prior to the competition.
Important Dates★	Student applications are due in late October. See guidelines for specific dates.
How to Enter★	Applications can be downloaded from the Web site. The application:

1. Must describe an individual community service activity or an individual's significant leadership in a group activity that has taken place during the previous year.
2. Must be completed and submitted to a school principal or the head of an officially designated organization by the last weekday in October.
3. Must be certified by the principal of a middle-level or high school or the head of an officially designated local organization.

Judging Criteria★	Judges consider students' project, inspiration, effort, impact, and personal growth.
Judges★	A national board of prominent judges.
Winner Notification★	State winners are notified in March; national winners are honored in May.

Awards★

Local honorees receive a certificate of recognition from their schools or organizations. State honorees receive an award of $1,000, an engraved silver medallion, and an all-expenses-paid trip to Washington, DC, for national recognition events. National honorees receive an additional award of $5,000, an engraved gold medallion, and a trophy for their school or organization.

Competition★	**Reflections Cultural Arts Program**
Sponsor★	The National PTA 330 N. Wabash Ave., Ste. 2100 Chicago, IL 60611
Web Address★	http://www.pta.org/parentinvolvement
Areas★	Language arts, performing arts, and visual arts
Competition Origin★	1969
Purpose★	To provide opportunities for students in preschool through the 12th grade to express and share their creative abilities. Each year, works of art are inspired by a theme, which is chosen from hundreds of student theme entries.
Description★	Students are encouraged to create and submit works of art in four areas: literature, musical composition, photography, and the visual arts (which includes art forms such as drawing, painting, print making, and collage). Guidelines are available from the state PTA or on the Web site.
Eligibility★	Students in grades Pre-K–12. There are four grade divisions: Primary (Pre-K–2); Intermediate (3–5); Middle/Junior (6–8); and Senior (9–12). Any PTA/PTSA in good standing may sponsor the Reflections Program.
Important Dates★	Contact state PTA for dates.
How to Enter★	See guidelines for details.
Judging Criteria★	Participation encourages creativity and exploration. Students should do their best; however, crooked lines, incorrect musical notes, or misspelled words do not disqualify anyone.
Judges★	Professionals working in literature, musical composition, photography, and visual arts fields volunteer to judge student entries at the national level.
Winner Notification★	All state PTAs are notified of national award recipients in late April and the National PTA sends award notification letters directly to students
Awards★	Three Awards of Excellence and five Awards of Merit are selected in each grade division for each of the four arts areas. In addition, one national Outstanding Interpretation work is chosen from

among the Awards of Excellence in each arts area. These students receive a trip to National PTA's Annual Convention for themselves and one adult chaperone. At the convention, the Outstanding Interpretation award recipients are recognized for their achievement and share their talents at a special awards presentation.

Advice★

Each entry must be the work of one student. Each student and his or her parent or guardian must sign the affirmation sentence on the official entry form stating that the entry is original. Artwork may be created in or outside of school.

★ ★

Competition★	**The Scholastic Writing and Art Awards**
Sponsor★	The Scholastic Writing and Art Awards 557 Broadway New York, NY 10012
Web Address★	http://www.scholastic.com/artandwritingawards
Areas★	Language arts and visual arts
Competition Origin★	1923
Purpose★	To recognize and encourage outstanding writing by students.
Description★	This is the National Writing Awards Program, the nation's largest and longest-running writing competition. There are a variety of competitions available for students. Check the Web site in October for new guidelines and deadlines.
Eligibility★	Students in grades 7–12. The portfolio competitions are for graduating seniors.
Important Dates★	Check the Web site in October for the latest competition details.
How to Enter★	You can obtain an entry form online or by writing to the sponsor.
Judging Criteria★	Writing awards are based upon technical proficiency, style, emergence of writer's voice, and originality. Art awards vary with each competition.
Judges★	Panels of qualified writers, editors, and educators.
Winner Notification★	Varies with each competition.
Awards★	More than 600 art awards and 300 writing awards are presented annually on the national level. Winners may receive cash awards, scholarships, certificates, and publishing and exhibition opportunities.
Advice★	Originality is essential to winning. Be sure to check the Web site for details for each competition in your region, as deadlines and requirements vary.

Competition★	**Science Olympiad**
Sponsor★	Science Olympiad 5955 Little Pine Lane Rochester, MI 48306
Web Address★	http://www.soinc.org
Areas★	Mathematics, science, and technology
Competition Origin★	1984
Purpose★	To challenge students to reach for higher goals and aspirations; to increase the interest of pre-college students in science, mathematics, and technology so that high-tech careers are an option as the students matriculate into institutions of higher education; and to wrap these serious intents into a context of a fun, exciting activity.
Description★	The Science Olympiad is an international non-profit organization devoted to improving the quality of science education, increasing student interest in science, and providing recognition for outstanding achievement in science education by both students and teachers. The Science Olympiad tournaments are rigorous academic, interscholastic competitions that consist of a series of 32 individual and team events, which students prepare for during the year. The competitions follow the format of popular board games, TV shows, and athletic games. The Rules Manual and Coaches Guide are available from the national offices or can be downloaded online.
Eligibility★	Students in grades K–12. The Olympiad has four grade divisions: A1 (K–3); A2 (3–6); B (6–9); and C (9–12). Only Divisions B and C have state, regional, and national competitions. Division A (A1 or A2) has only local or district activities.
Important Dates★	Each local, district, county, and state sets its own dates for competitions. The National Tournament is generally held during the third weekend in May. Since attendance at the National Tournament requires placement at state tournaments, states generally hold their competitions no later than mid-April. See guidelines for specific dates.
How to Enter★	Contact the national office for advice on registering.

Judging Criteria★   Judging criteria vary from event to event.

Judges★   Each tournament site is responsible for finding local judges with the technical expertise to judge the activity. This is the reason that many tournaments are held at college or university sites.

Winner Notification★   At all tournaments an awards ceremony is held and winners are named.

Awards★   Trophies are given to schools, winning coaches get plaques, and students receive Olympic-style medals.

Competition★	The Scripps Howard National Spelling Bee
Sponsor★	Scripps Howard National Spelling Bee 312 Walnut St., 28th Floor Cincinnati, OH 45202
Web Address★	http://www.spellingbee.com
Area★	Language arts
Competition Origin★	1925
Purpose★	To help students improve their spelling, increase their vocabularies, acquire concepts, learn language development, and improve reading skills that will benefit them their entire lives.
Description★	The program takes place on two levels: local and national. The only way students may participate in the National Spelling Bee is through an authorized sponsor in their area. The majority of sponsors are either daily, weekly, or Sunday newspapers. Authorized sponsors organize programs in their locales, often in cooperation with educators, businesses, and community organizations. These sponsors send their champions to the national finals. Guidelines may be obtained on the Web site or by writing to the sponsor.
Eligibility★	Students in grade 8 and under.
Important Dates★	The 2-day national competition is held on Wednesday and Thursday of the week in which Memorial Day is celebrated. See guidelines for specific dates.
How to Enter★	Contact the local authorized sponsor.
Judging Criteria★	The Scripps Howard National Spelling Bee is an oral competition conducted in rounds until only one speller remains. Each speller has been assigned a number and will spell in this order. A speller who correctly spells his or her word stays seated on the stage and waits for the next round. If the speller misspells his or her given word, that speller is eliminated from the competition.
Judges★	Appointed at local and national level by sponsors.
Winner Notification★	Winners are announced upon completion of each level of competition.

Awards★

The first-place winner receives a $12,000 cash prize and an engraved loving cup trophy from Scripps Howard Inc., choice of the Anniversary Edition of the *New Encyclopedia Britannica* or the *Great Books of the Western World* from Encyclopedia Britannica, and a $1,000 U.S. Savings Bond from Merriam-Webster. The second-place prize is $5,000. The third-place prize is $3,500.

Competition★	**SeaWorld/Busch Gardens/Fujifilm Environmental Excellence Awards**
Sponsor★	SeaWorld/Busch Gardens/Fujifilm Environmental Excellence Awards c/o SeaWorld Orlando Education Department 7007 SeaWorld Drive Orlando, FL 32821
Web Address★	http://www.seaworld.org/conservation-matters/eea
Areas★	Science and service learning
Competition Origin★	1993
Purpose★	The awards recognize the outstanding efforts of students, teachers, and community leaders across the country who are working at the grassroots level to protect and preserve the environment.
Description★	Students develop a project that shows their work in protecting and preserving the environment. Schools can obtain entry forms and guidelines from the Web site.
Eligibility★	Students in grades K–12.
Important Dates★	Deadline for entry is late November. See guidelines for specific dates.
How to Enter★	Submit application and 15-page project defense via mail by the deadline. Groups may submit photographs, videos, and other multimedia products to support the application. Obtain the application from the Web site.
Judging Criteria★	Judges look for the following:

- Project goals, objectives, and accomplishments;
- Project support/recognition;
- Impacts on students, school, community, and the environment;
- Proposed use of award money (how will it benefit the project?);
- Level of student/volunteer/citizen involvement and initiative;
- Originality/creativity;
- Support materials (photos, videos, articles); and
- General presentation of the application (organization, neatness).

Judges★

Projects are judged by representatives from SeaWorld, Busch Gardens, and Fujifilm, as well as representatives from their nine conservation and education partners.

Winner Notification★

All winners are notified by mail upon completion of the judging process.

Awards★

Eight projects are selected and receive $10,000 to benefit the award-winning project; an all-expenses-paid trip for three students and one adult leader to a SeaWorld or Busch Gardens park for a special awards event; a Fujifilm digital camera for use by award-winning group; 100 T-shirts to share with school and community partners; and award trophy and certificates for every student/group leader participant.

Advice★

Individual students (i.e., science fair projects) and previous award winning projects are not eligible to apply. Make sure you prepare a defense for each of the specific judging criteria.

Competition★	**Senior High Communication Contest**
Sponsor★	American Automobile Association 1000 AAA Dr. Heathrow, FL 32746-5063
Web Address★	http://www.aaasouth.com/ts_contest.asp
Area★	Visual arts
Competition Origin★	1996
Purpose★	To teach and promote traffic safety.
Description★	Senior high students have the opportunity to communicate their safety messages through other media (audio, video, brochures, editorials, cartoons, and computer art), as well as posters. There are 20 different traffic safety slogans, which are assigned to groups of states. Slogans are age-appropriate, such as *Occupant Protection*. Schools can obtain entry forms and guidelines at the beginning of the school year from their local AAA Club or from the Web site.
Eligibility★	Students in grades 9–12.
Important Dates★	Submit by early February. See guidelines for specific dates.
How to Enter★	Mail finished entry to either the main local office of AAA or to AAA National Headquarters.
Judging Criteria★	Posters and media materials are evaluated according to the following criteria: relationship of the design to traffic safety concepts, originality, how the idea is expressed in the design, and visual impact. Many AAA clubs conduct local or statewide judging prior to submitting posters to the national event.
Judges★	A panel of prominent individuals in the fields of education, art, and traffic safety.
Winner Notification★	Local AAA Clubs will notify the winners.
Awards★	First-, second-, and third-place are presented to top entrants. Winners share more than $18,400 in Visa Gift Checks. One Grand Award winner in the Senior High Communication Contest receives a $5,000 Visa Gift Check.

Competition★	**Spider's Corner**
Sponsor★	Spider's Corner P.O. Box 300 Peru, IL 61354
Web Address★	http://www.cricketmag.com/activity_display.asp?id=39
Areas★	Language arts and visual arts
Competition Origin★	1994
Purpose★	To encourage literary and artistic creativity and to provide a forum for personal expression.
Description★	Students are asked to draw or write about a theme usually drawn from a poem or story in a current issue of *Spider*. The themes and other guidelines are also available on the Web site.
Eligibility★	Students ages 6–9.
Important Dates★	Contest entries should be submitted by the 25th of each month.
How to Enter★	Entries must include the reader's name, age, and address and should be mailed to the sponsor.
Judging Criteria★	Stories, poems, and art are judged for their technique, originality, and adherence to contest themes and guidelines.
Judges★	The judges are members of *Spider*'s editorial and art departments.
Winner Notification★	Winners are notified 3–4 weeks after the deadline. The winning work is published within approximately 3 months of the contest deadline.
Awards★	Winning products are published in *Spider* magazine.
Advice★	Do not e-mail or fax entries. All entries must be signed by a parent or legal guardian, authorizing their publication in print and/or online and saying it's your own work and that no help was given.

Competition★	**Student Challenge Awards Program (SCAP)**
Sponsor★	Earth Watch Institute 3 Clock Tower Place, Ste. 100 P.O. Box 75 Maynard, MA 01754
Web Address★	http://www.earthwatch.org/education/student/scap/program.html
Area★	Science
Competition Origin★	1997
Purpose★	To encourage and stimulate the minds of students who are not very experienced in the field of science.
Description★	Students become part of a team, which includes other teens, graduate students, and scientists in hands-on scientific research projects. The program seeks gifted students with limited experience in the sciences. Students with limited resources and opportunities for enrichment are favored. Guidelines are available through the Web site.
Eligibility★	Students ages 16–18.
Important Dates★	Nomination forms are due in late December. See guidelines for specific dates.
How to Enter★	Students must be nominated by a teacher. Teachers may access entry forms through the Web site.
Judging Criteria★	Students must be motivated to learn, show leadership skills, communication skills, and should have the potential to make a difference.
Judges★	Nominees of the sponsor.
Winner Notification★	Winners are notified in March.
Awards★	The opportunity to work with a diverse research team lead by expert scientists. Awards cover the students' travel costs and their living expenses at the research site. Earthwatch Institute assigns award recipients to expeditions based on availability; disciplinary interests; travel enrichment; the physical demands of a project; team composition and compatibility; and the special interests of principal investigators.

Advice★

Nominators should keep in mind that this awards program does not aim to support the career development of future scientists, and may not emphasize a student's specific disciplinary interests when making project assignments.

★ ★

Competition★	**Student Electronic Music Composition Talent Search**
Sponsor★	The National Association for Music Education 1806 Robert Fulton Dr. Reston, VA 20901
Web Address★	http://www.menc.org/contest/nsba/nsbamain.html
Area★	Performing arts
Competition Origin★	2002
Purpose★	To recognize outstanding electronic music composition.
Description★	Teachers must submit an original student composition of 5 minutes or less. Compositions must be written with the use of electronic instrument(s) or other electronic media for manipulating sound, alone, or with any combination of vocal and/or acoustic instruments, live or recorded. Auxiliary support materials limited to one of the following: a 5 minute or fewer video; a 1,000 word or fewer essay; or a PowerPoint presentation printout of fewer than 30 slides. Composition must be part of a classroom curriculum and correspond to relevant standards. Visit the Web site to download guidelines and an application.
Eligibility★	Students in grades K–12. There are three grade divisions: Elementary (K–5); Middle level (6–8); and High School (grades 9–12).
Important Dates★	Entries are due in mid-April. See guidelines for specific dates.
How to Enter★	Download an entry form from the Web site and follow the instructions carefully. Your teacher must enter the composition on your behalf.
Judging Criteria★	Aesthetic quality, effective use of electronic media, and the power of the composition and its presentation in communicating to school board members, administrators, and others the excitement and effectiveness of electronic music composition in the school curriculum.
Judges★	Members of the National Association for Music Education.

Winner Notification★   Winners are posted on the Web site in July.

Awards★   Each winner receives "Sibelius" and "Photoscore Professional." Each winner's school receives the entire Sibelius educational suite of products (Notes, Starclass, Compass, Instruments, Auralia, Musition) and a Sibelius lab five-pack. To each winner's teacher goes a copy of *Composing and Arranging: Standard 4 Benchmarks, Composition in the Classroom: A Tool for Teaching,* and *Why and How to Teach Music Composition: A New Horizon for Music Education.* Five *Exploring General Music* keyboard lab student books and one teacher's score goes to each winner's school. Additional awards include a FUJIYAMA DVD and FUJIYAMA book with CD by Akira Jimbo on an organic approach to combining electronic and acoustic drums, using a Drum Trigger system to play melody, harmony, and rhythm.

Competition★	**Student Science Fiction and Fantasy Contest**
Sponsor★	Student Science Fiction Contest P.O. Box 314 Annapolis Junction, MD 20701
Web Address★	http://www.bucconeer.worldcon.org/contest/index.htm
Areas★	Language arts and visual arts
Competition Origin★	1996
Purpose★	To help young people understand that science fiction and fantasy expand horizons and open new worlds for their readers. The science of today, whether it is exploring the possibility of life on Mars or mapping the human genetic structure, can serve as the basis for science fiction stories.
Description★	The contest is for recognition of the best short story with a science fiction or fantasy theme, the best science fiction or fantasy artwork, and the best science essay written by 5th to 12th grade students. Each student may enter/win in any or all of the story, art, or essay categories, but may only enter once in each of the categories. Each entry must include a completed entry form. Guidelines may be obtained on the Web site or by writing to the sponsor.
Eligibility★	Students in grades 5–12.
Important Dates★	Entries must be postmarked by the end of March. See guidelines for specific dates.
How to Enter★	Complete the entry form at their Web address and mail it to the sponsor.
Judging Criteria★	Short story entries will be judged on their originality and creativity; grammar and spelling; structure; character development; plot development; and the use of science fiction and fantasy elements. Artwork entries will be judged on their originality and creativity, artistic technique, and the use of science fiction and fantasy elements. Science essay entries will be judged on content; grammar and spelling; structure; and use of references.
Judges★	Appointed by the sponsor.
Winner Notification★	Winners are announced at a special ceremony honoring the contestants at Noreascon in September.

Awards★

All contestants receive a certificate for participating. Semi-finalists are invited to attend Noreascon. Finalists also receive a commemorative T-shirt and a $10 gift certificate from a major book store. The winners are invited to attend all 5 days of Noreascon and receive a commemorative T-shirt and a $50 gift certificate from a major book store.

Competition★	**TEAMS (Tests of Engineering Aptitude, Mathematics, and Science)**
Sponsor★	Junior Engineering Technical Society Inc. (JETS) 1420 King St., Ste. 405 Alexandria, VA 22314
Web Address★	http://www.jets.org/programs/teams.cfm
Areas★	Engineering, mathematics, and science
Competition Origin★	1979
Purpose★	To help prepare students for tomorrow's world today.
Description★	Teams participate in an open-book, open-discussion environment to solve real-world engineering problems. Mathematics and science concepts taught in school are applied to real-world problems. TEAMS problems focus on all areas of mathematics and science, as well as on computer fundamentals, graphics interpretation, and English/communication skills and concepts. Information is updated each summer for the following year's TEAMS program. Information is available year-round from the sponsor or on the Web site.
Eligibility★	Students in grades 9–12.
Important Dates★	TEAMS is a 1-day, two-part event held between early February and mid-March each year. Schools may register teams beginning in September. See guidelines for specific dates.
How to Enter★	Schools that have not participated before should contact JETS for information on the competition site nearest them. All schools register directly with the competition host.
Judging Criteria★	Part 1 (multiple-choice): accuracy of answers. Part 2 (subjective portion): scored by a panel of engineers determined by JETS and the TEAMS problem development coordinator.
Judges★	The objective test is machine scored. Engineers and coordinators judge the subjective portion.
Winner Notification★	Teams usually receive local (regional) results on competition day. State rankings are announced 1 week after the last competition date. National rankings are announced by mid-April.

Awards★

Awards are given for regional, state, and national recognition. Regional and state awards vary by site and state; national awards are given by JETS and vary from year to year.

Advice★

Register early in order to receive coaching and preparation materials in time to make them useful.

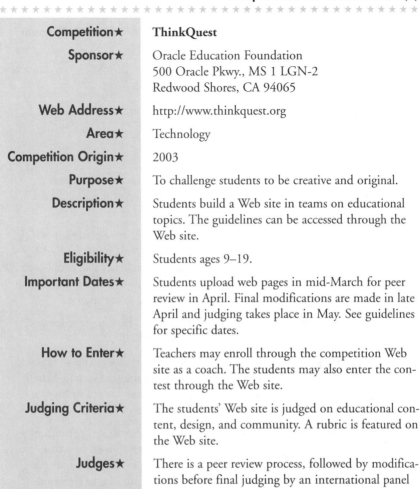

Competition★	**ThinkQuest**
Sponsor★	Oracle Education Foundation 500 Oracle Pkwy., MS 1 LGN-2 Redwood Shores, CA 94065
Web Address★	http://www.thinkquest.org
Area★	Technology
Competition Origin★	2003
Purpose★	To challenge students to be creative and original.
Description★	Students build a Web site in teams on educational topics. The guidelines can be accessed through the Web site.
Eligibility★	Students ages 9–19.
Important Dates★	Students upload web pages in mid-March for peer review in April. Final modifications are made in late April and judging takes place in May. See guidelines for specific dates.
How to Enter★	Teachers may enroll through the competition Web site as a coach. The students may also enter the contest through the Web site.
Judging Criteria★	The students' Web site is judged on educational content, design, and community. A rubric is featured on the Web site.
Judges★	There is a peer review process, followed by modifications before final judging by an international panel of education specialists.
Winner Notification★	Winners are notified at the end of May.
Awards★	The winning Web sites become part of the ThinkQuest Library and winners are invited to attend ThinkQuestLive!.

Competition★	**Toshiba/NSTA ExploraVision Awards Program**
Sponsor★	Toshiba/NSTA ExploraVision Awards 1840 Wilson Blvd. Arlington, VA 22201-3000
Web Address★	http://www.exploravision.org
Area★	Technology
Competition Origin★	1992
Purpose★	To provide opportunities for K–12 students to enhance or design technologies that could exist in the future.
Description★	This is the world's largest science contest in which teams of three to four students in grades K–12 expand on or design technologies that could exist 20 years in the future. Guidelines may be obtained on the Web site or by writing to the sponsor.
Eligibility★	Students in grades K–12. There are four grade divisions: K–3; 4–6; 7–9; and 10–12.
Important Dates★	The entry deadline is in February. The 48 regional semi-finalist teams are announced in mid-March. The 12 finalist teams are announced in May. See guidelines for specific dates.
How to Enter★	Teams must submit a teacher signed entry form, a 10 page or less typed description of their technology, and storyboards depicting scenes from a sample 5-minute video they would produce to convey their ideas.
Judging Criteria★	Decisions are based upon creativity, scientific accuracy, communication, and feasibility of vision.
Judges★	Leading science educators serve as judges.
Winner Notification★	Winners are notified in early June.
Awards★	Student members of the four first-place teams each receive a U.S. EE Savings Bond worth $10,000 at maturity. Second-place winners receive U.S. EE series bonds worth $5,000 at maturity. First- and second-place Canadian winners receive Canada savings bonds purchased for the equivalent issue price in Canadian dollars. National finalist team members and their parents/guardians travel to Washington, DC, in June for ExploraVision Awards Weekend

where they are recognized for their outstanding achievement. Each student on the 24 regional winning teams and honorable mention teams is recognized for their creative vision with a special gift. Every student team member who enters the competition with a complete entry receives a certificate of participation and a small gift. There are also prizes and recognition for coaches and mentors.

Advice★

The Web site answers many questions students may have and is filled with useful information.

Competition★	**UNA-USA National High School Essay Contest**
Sponsor★	United Nations Association of the United States of America 801 Second Ave. New York, NY 10017
Web Address★	http://www.unausa.org
Area★	Social studies
Competition Origin★	1986
Purpose★	To engage students in a serious research and writing exercise about the United Nations and the issues confronting the world organization and to broaden the perspectives of American students to better understand the complexities of our world and the challenges our nation faces as a member of the international community.
Description★	High school students write and submit essays on the United Nations. Guidelines may be obtained on the Web site or by writing to the sponsor.
Eligibility★	Students in grades 9–12.
Important Dates★	Entries are due in early January. UNA-USA announces each chapter winner in January, and national finalists are notified in late February. See guidelines for specific dates.
How to Enter★	To enter the program, teachers and students are encouraged to contact their local United Nations Association chapter or the sponsor. Chapter addresses and contact details are available on the Web site.
Judging Criteria★	Decisions are based upon research and writing, as well as demonstration of an understanding of the issue.
Judges★	National panel of experts.
Winner Notification★	Winners are notified in March.
Awards★	Cash awards of $3,000 (first prize), $1,500 (second prize), and $750 (third prize) and an all-expenses-paid trip for the prize-winning students and their teachers to New York City for the awards ceremony are awarded each year.

★ ★

Advice★
Remember, there are no right or wrong questions. The essay should reflect your perspective as a student.

Competition★	**United Nations Environmental Programme (UNEP) International Photographic Competition on the Environment**
Sponsor★	United Nations Environment Programme United Nations Ave., Gigiri P.O. Box 30552 00100, Nairobi, Kenya
Web Address★	http://www.unep-photo.com/en/outline/index.html
Areas★	Science and visual arts
Competition Origin★	2000
Purpose★	To make people of all ages aware of environmental challenges by giving an opportunity to express hope, joy, or anger regarding life on earth.
Description★	Students create a visual journal that depicts the many environmental challenges the Earth is facing. Guidelines may be obtained on the Web site or by writing to the sponsor.
Eligibility★	Open to people of all nationalities and ages. A children's category is for those up to age 14 and youth category for those 15–24.
Important Dates★	Photos are due biennially in October. See guidelines for specific dates.
How to Enter★	Contact sponsor for how to enter.
Judging Criteria★	Depiction of the theme for each contest.
Judges★	Photographers and representatives of the sponsors (UNEP and Canon).
Winner Notification★	Winners are notified in March.
Awards★	In the children's division, the first-place winner receives $2,000; the second-place winner receives $1,000; and the third-place winner receives $500. Winners and honorable mentions also receive plaques. For the youth division, the first-place winner receives $5,000; the second-place winner receives $2,000; and the third-place winner receives $1,000. Winners and honorable mentions also receive plaques. Prize winning photographs are displayed at the awards ceremony and may travel internationally for similar events.

Advice★   All travel costs for the awards ceremony are the winners' responsibility.

Competition★	**United Nations Pilgrimage for Youth**
Sponsor★	United Nations Pilgrimage for Youth, Inc. Independent Order of Odd Fellows 422 Trade Street Winston-Salem, North Carolina 27101-2830
Web Address★	http://www.onlinedemocracy.ca/community/ioof.html
Area★	Social studies
Competition Origin★	1950
Purpose★	To study and learn about the United Nations.
Description★	Students complete a U.N. exam, submit an essay, and/or participate in a speech contest. Contact your local Odd Fellow and/or Rebekah Lodges for more information.
Eligibility★	Students ages 16–17.
Important Dates★	Dates vary. Contact your local Odd Fellow Lodge for an application.
How to Enter★	Contact local Odd Fellow and/or Rebekah Lodges.
Judging Criteria★	Applications are reviewed by selecting committees for evidence of scholarship, leadership, character, extra-curricular activities, concern for community welfare, interest in world affairs, and general fitness to participate in the program.
Judges★	Members of the Independent Order of Odd Fellows and Rebekahs.
Winner Notification★	Winners are notified prior to summer.
Awards★	Winners tour the United Nations building and listen to behind-the-scenes briefings conducted by special-ized United Nations agencies and departments, as well as visit other sights in New York City. Expenses including transportation, meals, lodging, and sight-seeing are paid for by the Odd Fellow and Rebekah lodges in your community, county, district, state, or province and donations by corporations and individ-uals. The student provides spending money for sou-venirs, laundry, shopping, extra refreshments, and some entertainment.

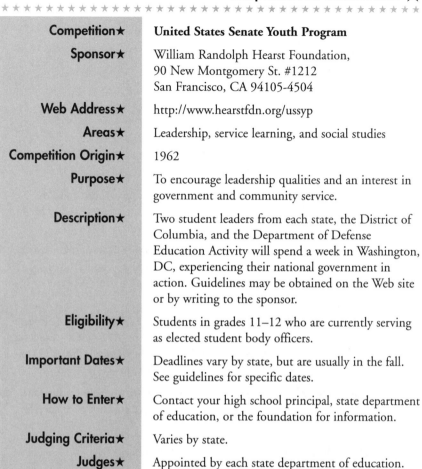

Competition★	**United States Senate Youth Program**
Sponsor★	William Randolph Hearst Foundation, 90 New Montgomery St. #1212 San Francisco, CA 94105-4504
Web Address★	http://www.hearstfdn.org/ussyp
Areas★	Leadership, service learning, and social studies
Competition Origin★	1962
Purpose★	To encourage leadership qualities and an interest in government and community service.
Description★	Two student leaders from each state, the District of Columbia, and the Department of Defense Education Activity will spend a week in Washington, DC, experiencing their national government in action. Guidelines may be obtained on the Web site or by writing to the sponsor.
Eligibility★	Students in grades 11–12 who are currently serving as elected student body officers.
Important Dates★	Deadlines vary by state, but are usually in the fall. See guidelines for specific dates.
How to Enter★	Contact your high school principal, state department of education, or the foundation for information.
Judging Criteria★	Varies by state.
Judges★	Appointed by each state department of education.
Winner Notification★	Generally, winners are notified in December.
Awards★	$5,000 college scholarships and all-expenses-paid week in Washington, DC.
Advice★	Students should start exploring participation in this program soon after the school year begins.

Competition★	**U.S. Academic Decathlon**
Sponsor★	U.S. Academic Decathlon P.O. Box 1868 10604 Los Alamitos Blvd. Los Alamitos, CA 90720-1868
Web Address★	http://www.usad.org
Area★	Academic quiz bowl
Competition Origin★	1981
Purpose★	To improve the status, the recognition, and the popularity of academic endeavor in every high school in the U.S.
Description★	The Academic Decathlon is a 10-event scholastic competition for teams of high school students. Guidelines may be obtained on the Web site or by writing to the sponsor.
Eligibility★	Students in grades 9–12. Each high school enters a team of nine students: three "A" or Honor students; three "B" or Scholastic students; and three "C" or Varsity students.
Important Dates★	Local and state competitions are held prior to the national finals in April. See guidelines for specific dates.
How to Enter★	See the Web site for details.
Judging Criteria★	Accuracy of answers.
Judges★	Volunteers and company personnel manage the process of scoring.
Winner Notification★	Winners are notified at the national finals in April.
Awards★	Gold, silver, and bronze medals are awarded for individual events and total scores.
Advice★	Study materials and resource guides are available for purchase on the Web site. It is important to contact local and state sponsors to ensure that deadlines are met for participation.

★ ★

Competition★	**U.S. National Chemistry Olympiad**
Sponsor★	American Chemical Society 1155 16th St. NW Washington, DC 20036
Web Address★	http://www.chemistry.org
Area★	Science
Competition Origin★	1984
Purpose★	To promote excellence in chemistry, as well as to select four students to represent the United States at the International Chemistry Olympiad.
Description★	The U.S. National Chemistry Olympiad (USNCO) is a multi-tiered competition for high school students. The local section competitions are usually held from late February to early April and consist of a locally determined competition such as a written exam, a laboratory practical, or a science fair. The best students from the local competition participate in the three-part national exam in late April. The national exam consists of a 60-question multiple-choice section, an eight-question free-response section, and a two-exercise laboratory practical. Guidelines may be obtained on the Web site or by writing to the sponsor.
Eligibility★	Students in grades 9–12 who are enrolled in chemistry.
Important Dates★	Local competitions are held February through April, and the national exam is given in late April. See guidelines for specific dates.
How to Enter★	Students should discuss entry with their chemistry teacher who can register by contacting the sponsor.
Judging Criteria★	Accuracy of answers.
Judges★	Teachers and chemists.
Winner Notification★	Winners are announced on-site for national and international competitions.
Awards★	Of the approximately 1,000 students taking this exam, 20 are invited to attend a 2-week study camp, held at the U.S. Air Force Academy in mid-June. At the study camp, the students undergo an intense schedule of lectures, laboratory exercises, and exams.

The top four students are selected from the camp to compete in the International Chemistry Olympiad in mid-July.

Competition★	**USA Biology Olympiad (USABO)**
Sponsor★	Center for Excellence in Education 8201 Greensboro Dr., Ste. 215 McLean, VA 22102
Web Address★	http://www.cee.org/usabo
Area★	Science
Competition Origin★	1960s
Purpose★	To motivate high school students' curiosity about the different fields of biology. This competition also focuses on challenging students and allowing them to experience competitive opportunities.
Description★	This is a four level competition that consists of multiple-choice questions, short answers, and group competitions. Teachers begin by registering their biology class. This can be done through the USABO Web site. Guidelines are sent after this step is completed.
Eligibility★	Students in grades 9–12 who are enrolled in biology.
Important Dates★	Registration is from November to January. The open exam is in January and the semifinals will be held in March. The fourth round of the competition is held in mid-July. See guidelines for specific dates.
How to Enter★	Have your biology teacher visit the Web site and register your class.
Judging Criteria★	Accuracy of answers.
Judges★	Teachers and USABO officials.
Winner Notification★	Winners are notified at each level of competition.
Awards★	Medals are distributed and advancement to the National and International Biology Olympiad is granted to winners.
Advice★	The Web site offers sample exams linked to other Web sites. There are also other textbook listings and material provided for studying.

Competition★	**USA Computing Olympiad (USACO)**
Sponsor★	University of Wisconsin-Parkside 900 Wood Road Kenosha, WI 53141-2000
Web Address★	http://oldweb.uwp.edu/academic/mathematics/usaco
Areas★	Creativity/problem solving and technology
Competition Origin★	1992
Purpose★	To select the team of four students to represent the United States in the annual International Olympiad in Informatics (IOI).
Description★	The goals of the USACO are to provide U.S. students with opportunities to sharpen their computing skills, enabling them to compete successfully at the international level; enhance the quality of computer education in U.S. high schools by providing students and teachers with challenging programming problems that emphasize algorithm development and problem solving skills; and select the U.S. team to attend the annual International Olympiad in Informatics. Students progress through a number of rounds in which they must successfully answer different programming problems. Information about the USACO and IOI is available from the sponsor and on the Web site.
Eligibility★	Students in grades 6–12.
Important Dates★	Contests are held in December, January, February, and March, with the national competition in April. See guidelines for specific dates.
How to Enter★	Contact a high school or college teacher who will serve as a local coordinator. Have the local coordinator contact the USACO or sign up online at the Web site.
Judging Criteria★	The winners are selected based on their performance at the final round of the USACO.
Judges★	The staff of the USACO serves as judges.
Winner Notification★	The USA team is notified at the April competition.
Awards★	The 16 finalists in the Competition Round receive an all-expenses-paid trip to a week-long training camp. Four students selected for the USACO team

receive an all-expenses-paid trip to the International Olympiad in Informatics which is held in a different country each year and lasts for 10 days.

Competition★	**USA Mathematical Talent Search (USAMTS)**
Sponsor★	USA Mathematical Talent Search P.O. Box 2090 Alpine, CA 91903-2090
Web Address★	http://www.usamts.org
Area★	Mathematics
Competition Origin★	1989
Purpose★	To encourage and assist the development of problem solving skills of talented high school students.
Description★	Most competitions require students to answer several questions over a few hours, often in multiple-choice format. The USAMTS is different in that students have a full month to work out their solutions. Carefully written justifications are required for each problem. Each year, the USAMTS consists of four rounds, each round featuring five problems. The problems are published on the USAMTS Web site. Each round of problems is published to allow at least 4 weeks for solution. Students are asked to submit solutions to at least two of the problems each round. They can earn 5 points for the complete, well-written solution of each problem, and hence can accumulate 100 points during the school year. Guidelines may be obtained on the Web site or by writing to the sponsor.
Eligibility★	Students in grades 6–12.
Important Dates★	Solutions are due in early October, November, January, and March. Check the Web site for dates. See guidelines for specific dates.
How to Enter★	Visit the Web site for details and your entry application.
Judging Criteria★	Accuracy of answers.
Judges★	USAMTS officials.
Winner Notification★	At the end of each round, in addition to the solutions and a copy of the completed individual USAMTS cover sheet, each participant receives a copy of a newsletter, which provides an update on the competition, as well as other valuable information.

Awards★

Certificates and book prizes are given to gold, silver, and bronze winners, and prizes are given for honorable mention winners.

Competition★	*USA Today* **John Lennon Songwriting Contest for Teens**
Sponsor★	*USA WEEKEND*-John Lennon Songwriting Contest for Teens P.O. Box 8521 Prospect Heights, IL 60070
Web Address★	http://www.usaweekend.com/classroom/song_entry.html
Area★	Performing arts
Competition Origin★	2003
Purpose★	To give students the opportunity to express their views through songwriting.
Description★	Students write original song lyrics that reflect the selected theme. Visit the Web site for guidelines.
Eligibility★	Students in grades 7–12 and at least 13 years of age.
Important Dates★	Deadline for entry is in February. See guidelines for specific dates.
How to Enter★	Mail your entry or submit it online.
Judging Criteria★	All judging is based on the following criteria: originality and creativity (40%); songwriting ability (30%); and appropriateness of song lyrics for recording (30%).
Judges★	Appointed by *USA Weekend*.
Winner Notification★	Finalists are selected in mid-April and grand prize winners are notified in May.
Awards★	Prizes include a trip and U.S. savings bonds. See Web site for details.
Advice★	Entries must be the original work of the entrant, written in English, and must not exceed a total of 125 words in length (including the song title). All entries, including the copy of entrants' song lyrics, become property of the sponsor, and none will be returned. Only one entry per person.

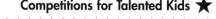
Competition★	**The Vegetarian Resource Group Essay**
Sponsor★	The Vegetarian Resource Group P.O. Box 1463 Baltimore, MD 21203
Web Address★	http://www.vrg.org/essay
Area★	Language arts
Competition Origin★	1996
Purpose★	To emphasize the ethics, culture, health, aesthetics, economics, and environmental issues that are involved with vegetarianism.
Description★	Students write a 2–3 page essay on any issue related to vegetarianism. Guidelines are available through the Web site.
Eligibility★	Students in grades K–12. There are three age divisions: 8 and under; 9–13; and 14–18.
Important Dates★	Entries must be postmarked by early May. See guidelines for specific dates.
How to Enter★	Mail essay to the sponsor's address or e-mail from the Web site.
Judging Criteria★	Entries are judged based on personal opinion, research, and interviews.
Judges★	Staff of The Vegetarian Resource Group.
Winner Notification★	Winners are notified by mail upon completion of judging.
Awards★	A $50 savings bond is awarded to the winner in each age division. The winning essays are also posted on the Web site.
Advice★	You need not be a vegetarian to enter. All essays become the property of The Vegetarian Resource Group.

Competition★	**Very Special Arts Playwright Discovery Award for Students**
Sponsor★	VSA Playwright Discovery Award for Students 1300 Connecticut Avenue, NW, Ste. 700 Washington, DC 20036
Web Address★	http://www.vsarts.org
Area★	Language arts and performing arts
Competition Origin★	2002
Purpose★	To challenge middle and high school students of all abilities to take a closer look at the world around them, examine how disability affects their lives and the lives of others, and express their views through the art of writing a one-act play.
Description★	Students write a one-act play that expresses how disability affects their lives and the lives of others. Guidelines may be obtained on the Web site or by writing to the sponsor.
Eligibility★	Students in grades 6–12, regardless of ability.
Important Dates★	Plays should be submitted by mid-April. See guidelines for specific dates.
How to Enter★	Download an application form from the Web site.
Judging Criteria★	Scripts must somehow address the issue of disability. The disability may be visible (e.g., a character who is blind or uses a wheelchair) or hidden (e.g., a character with a learning or emotional disability). Submissions must be appropriate in language and subject matter for middle and high school audiences.
Judges★	A distinguished jury of award-winning theater professionals selects the winning scripts.
Winner Notification★	Winners are notified prior to the awards recognition ceremony, which is held in September or October each year.
Awards★	Two scripts are selected for professional production or staged reading at The John F. Kennedy Center for the Performing Arts., and award recipients receive scholarship funds and a trip to Washington, DC, to view the production or reading. This includes round trip coach travel, double hotel room, and per diem; a mentoring luncheon with distinguished members of

the Artists Selection Committee; press opportunities; and a scholarship award in the amount of $1,000 per selected script.

Advice★

The sponsor suggests: "Write a play. Twist reality. Twist truths. Shatter expectations. Shatter perceptions. Invent worlds. Invent people. Startle people. Startle yourself. Transport your audience. Transport your mind. Make us laugh. Write a play."

Competition★	**Voice of Democracy**
Sponsor★	The Veterans of Foreign Wars of the United States and its Ladies Auxiliary VFW Building 406 W. 34th St. Kansas City, MO 06411
Web Address★	http://www.vfw.org
Area★	Language arts
Competition Origin★	1946
Purpose★	To allow students the opportunity to voice opinions on a patriotic theme.
Description★	Students compete for prizes and money with winners selected based upon an audio essay. This is an essay recorded on a cassette tape as read by the student. The theme varies each year; for example, the theme for the 2005 contest was "How I Demonstrate My Freedom." Contact the local VFW Post or Auxiliary for guidelines or visit the Web site.
Eligibility★	Students in grades 10–12.
Important Dates★	Entry deadline is in early November. See guidelines for specific dates.
How to Enter★	Contact sponsor for official rules. The Web site includes guidelines for entry and an entry form that can be downloaded.
Judging Criteria★	Originality, content, and delivery.
Judges★	Judges are selected by VFW and include representatives from the major broadcast networks and government officials.
Winner Notification★	Winners are announced in March at the annual Veterans of Foreign Wars Washington Conference.
Awards★	Each Department's first-place winner receives an all-expenses-paid trip to Washington, DC, plus the opportunity to compete for national scholarships. The first-place national winner receives a $25,000 scholarship.
Advice★	Carefully read guidelines for details.

Competition★	**Washington Crossing Foundation Scholarship Awards**
Sponsor★	Washington Crossing Foundation P.O. Box 503 Levittown, PA 19058
Web Address★	http://www.gwcf.org/applicants/awards.htm
Area★	Social Studies
Competition Origin★	1969
Purpose★	To provide students who are planning careers in government service an opportunity to express their career plans.
Description★	Each interested student is invited to write a one–page essay stating why he or she plans a career in government service including any inspiration to be derived from the leadership of George Washington in his famous crossing of the Delaware. Applications are sent to all high schools in the United States in September each year. Details are also available on the Web site.
Eligibility★	Students in grade 12 who are interested in going into government work.
Important Dates★	Applications must be submitted to the foundation by mid-January. See guidelines for specific dates.
How to Enter★	Request an application from the Washington Crossing Foundation or download the information from the Web site.
Judging Criteria★	The judges' decision will be based on understanding of career requirements, purpose in choice of a career, qualities of leadership exhibited, sincerity, and historical perspective. Semi-finalists may be interviewed by telephone as part of the selection process. All finalists will be interviewed by telephone.
Judges★	The board of judges consists of at least three trustees of the Foundation, one member of the Washington Crossing Park Commission, and a prominent educator.
Winner Notification★	Winners will be notified by telephone in April, with confirmation by mail.

★ ★

Awards★

The first-place award of $5,000 is the Ann Hawkes Hutton Scholarship. The second-place award of $5,000 is the I.J. Schekter Scholarship. The third-place award of $5,000 is the Frank and Katharine Davis Scholarship. Each award is paid over a period of 4 years, if the student meets the requirements of the college chosen, maintains a suitable scholastic level, and continues his or her career objective. Other state and regional awards may be available.

. Advice★

Applicants with full 4-year tuition scholarships are only eligible for 1-year special awards.

★ ★

Competition★	**We the People: The Citizen and the Constitution**
Sponsor★	Center for Civic Education 5145 Douglas Fir Rd. Calabasas, CA 91302-1440
Web Address★	http://www.civiced.org/wethepeople.php
Area★	Social studies
Competition Origin★	1987
Purpose★	To promote civic competence and responsibility among students.
Description★	Upon completion of the curriculum, teachers involve their entire class in a simulated congressional hearing. A model of performance assessment, the hearing provides an excellent culminating activity and an opportunity for students to demonstrate their knowledge and understanding of the principles of the Constitution and Bill of Rights. Information may be obtained on the Web site or by writing to the sponsor.
Eligibility★	Classes in grades 9–12.
Important Dates★	Interested teachers contact the coordinator for the congressional district their school is in and request instructional material in August or September. District-level hearings are held in November–January. State-level hearings are held in January–March, and the national-level hearings are held in April or May. See guidelines for specific dates.
How to Enter★	Have your teacher contact the Center for Civic Education and request the name of the state and district coordinator for the congressional district in which your school is located.
Judging Criteria★	At the district level, the judges score the students' performance on the basis of their knowledge and understanding of the Constitution and Bill of Rights and their ability to apply constitutional principles to historical and contemporary issues. Classes earning the highest scores go on to a state level hearing. Oral presentations, before another panel of judges, are based on a new set of hearing and follow-up questions. Each judge scores each group (unit) on a scale

of 1–10 (10 being the highest) in six categories using a "Congressional Hearing Group Score Sheet." These six categories are: understanding, constitutional application, reasoning, supporting evidence, responsiveness, and participation.

Judges★

At the district level, district coordinators select community members and individuals who have professional background and/or experience with the Constitution (e.g., lawyers, professors, government officials). At the state level, judges are selected who have professional experience with the Constitution and experience serving as judges at the district level. At the national level, judges are nominated by state coordinators.

Winner Notification★

District and state winning classes are announced at the end of the scheduled competitive hearing event. Winning classes are announced at an awards banquet in Washington, DC, at the end of a 3-day nation-level hearing.

Awards★

At district and state, awards for first, second, and third place are distributed. A Certificate of Achievement is awarded to each school. Awards are given for outstanding performance in each of the six unit topics. Plaques are given to the seven teams placing fourth through tenth. Classes placing first, second, and third receive national recognition from adults and peers at the Gala Awards Banquet. Teachers and students also receive medallions.

Advice★

Teachers who participate in the competition thoroughly teach the We the People curriculum. Competing classes are often coached by lawyers, professors, and other professionals.

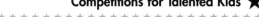
Competition★	**The WordMasters Challenge**
Sponsor★	WordMasters 213 E. Allendale Ave. Allendale, NJ 07401
Web Address★	http://www.wordmasterschallenge.com
Area★	Language arts
Competition Origin★	1987
Purpose★	To encourage growth in vocabulary and verbal reasoning.
Description★	Students are challenged to complete analogies based on relationships among the words they have learned through vocabulary development. The contest consists of three 20-minute analogy-solving contests. Guidelines may be obtained on the Web site or by writing to the sponsor.
Eligibility★	Students in grades 3–12. There are two grade divisions: Vocabulary and Analogies (3–8) and Analytical Reading (9–12).
Important Dates★	Meets are scheduled during December, February, and April. See guidelines for specific dates.
How to Enter★	Schools wishing to participate must register and pay an entrance fee to the sponsor by mid-October.
Judging Criteria★	Accuracy of answers.
Judges★	Participating teachers and WordMasters officials.
Winner Notification★	Winners are notified at the conclusion of each academic year.
Awards★	Medal and certificates of merit.

Competition★	**Yoshiyama Award for Exemplary Service to the Community**
Sponsor★	The Yoshiyama Award 1509 22nd St. NW Washington, DC 20037-1073
Web Address★	http://www.hitachifoundation.org/yoshiyama
Areas★	Leadership and service learning
Competition Origin★	1988
Purpose★	To recognize high school seniors who have distinguished themselves through extensive service and leadership in their communities.
Description★	This award is given annually to 6–10 high school seniors selected from throughout the United States on the basis of their community service activities. Guidelines may be obtained on the Web site or by writing to the sponsor.
Eligibility★	Students in grade 12 (rising and graduating).
Important Dates★	Nomination packets must be postmarked by early April. See guidelines for specific dates.
How to Enter★	Complete the nomination form, letter of nomination, and two supporting letters. Applicants must be nominated; self-nominations and family nominations are automatically disqualified.
Judging Criteria★	Community service, self-motivation, leadership, creativity, dedication, and commitment.
Judges★	National panel of outstanding leaders, representing various professions, but all committed to the development of leadership and civic responsibility.
Winner Notification★	Winners are notified in August or September.
Awards★	$5,000 gift, dispensed over 2 years, to be used at the discretion of award recipients and an invitation to a special award ceremony and retreat in Washington, DC.
Advice★	Students may not nominate themselves. This is not a scholarship program.

★ ★

Competition★	**Young American Creative Patriotic Art Contest**
Sponsor★	Ladies Auxiliary VFW National Headquarters 406 West 34th St. Kansas City, MO 64111
Web Address★	http://www.ladiesauxvfw.com
Area★	Visual arts
Competition Origin★	1978
Purpose★	To promote patriotism among youth in the United States.
Description★	Students submit a piece of art on paper or canvas that is matted. Water color, pencil, pastel, charcoal, tempera, crayon, acrylic, pen-and-ink, or oil may be used. Guidelines can be obtained on the Web site or by contacting your state chapter.
Eligibility★	Students in grades 9–12.
Important Dates★	Students should submit their artwork to state chapters by the end of March. The national competition is held in May. See guidelines for specific dates.
How to Enter★	Students must enter at state level first. Winners from each state compete in the national competition. Contact your state's chapter for local deadlines.
Judging Criteria★	Each entry is judged on the originality of concept, presentation, and patriotism expressed; the content of how it relates to patriotism and clarity of ideas; the design technique; the total impact of work; and uniqueness.
Judges★	Those selected to judge the contest on all levels are teachers, professionals, and persons knowledgeable in art.
Winner Notification★	Winners are notified prior to the September national meeting.
Awards★	State prizes may vary. National scholarships of $10,000, $5,000, and $2,500 are awarded to first-, second-, and third-place winners respectively. Also, first prize includes a jacket, a plaque, and airfare, plus two nights lodging to attend the Ladies Auxiliary National Convention. The winning art is unveiled at the Convention and featured on the cover of the National VFW Auxiliary Magazine and

on the Auxiliary Web site. Second- and third-place winning entries in the National Contest are featured in the National VFW Auxiliary Magazine and on the Auxiliary Web site.

Competition★	**Young Game Inventors Contest**
Sponsor★	University Games Corporate 2030 Harrison St. San Francisco, CA 94110
Web Address★	http://www.ugames.com
Area★	Creativity/problem solving
Competition Origin★	1993
Purpose★	To provide students an opportunity to apply their creativity in designing and inventing their own board games.
Description★	Students create an original board game, including rules and game board. Guidelines may be obtained on the Web site or by writing to the sponsor.
Eligibility★	Children ages 5–12.
Important Dates★	Entries must be postmarked in early November. See guidelines for specific dates.
How to Enter★	Submit game and entry form to sponsor. The entry form can be downloaded from the Web site.
Judging Criteria★	Judges look for a fun game and a creative idea. Entries are judged based on concept, not artwork.
Judges★	University Games Officials.
Winner Notification★	Winners are notified by mail.
Awards★	The grand-prize winner receives a $10,000 savings bond, trip to San Francisco, a game library from University Games, and a chance to have their game produced by University Games. Runners-up receive a game library from University Games.
Advice★	Only one entry per child is accepted and it must be signed by a parent or guardian.

Competition★	**Young Naturalist Awards**
Sponsor★	National Center for Science Literacy, Education, and Technology, American Museum of Natural History Central Park West at 79th St. New York, NY 10024-5192
Web Address★	http://www.amnh.org/nationalcenter/youngnaturalistawards
Areas★	Language arts and science
Competition Origin★	1998
Purpose★	To encourage students to participate and interact with science.
Description★	Students write a research based narrative essay on a certain topic. They explore and collect data on this topic. Guidelines may be obtained on the Web site or by writing to the sponsor.
Eligibility★	Students in grades 7–12.
Important Dates★	Students may start submitting entries as early June with all entries due in early January. See guidelines for specific dates.
Judging Criteria★	Entries are judged according to the student's investigation, procedure, analysis, interpretation, research materials, clarity of the report, and style of writing.
Judges★	Museum scientists.
Winner notification★	Winners are notified in the spring.
Awards★	Twelve winners receive cash scholarships and trips to New York City to meet museum scientists. Thirty-six finalists also receive cash awards, T-shirts, and certificates. Three hundred semifinalists receive various prizes and certificates. Teachers of winning students receive a collection of books for their classroom.

Competition★	**Young Playwrights Festival**
Sponsor★	Young Playwrights, Inc. 306 West 38th Street, #300 New York, NY 10018
Web Address★	http://www.youngplaywrights.org/nationalcontest.htm
Areas★	Language arts and performing arts
Competition Origin★	1981
Purpose★	To introduce young people to the theater and to encourage self-expression through the art of playwriting.
Description★	Students submit an original play that will be read and evaluated by a theater professional. Guidelines may be obtained on the Web site or by writing to the sponsor.
Eligibility★	Students ages 18 and younger (as of deadline).
Important Dates★	The deadline for entry is the beginning of December. See guidelines for specific dates.
How to Enter★	Obtain the guidelines and submit original playscript according to the guidelines. Screenplays and musicals are not eligible. More than one play may be submitted.
Judging Criteria★	Selections are based on the quality of writing in playwriting competition. Each playwright receives a written evaluation of the work submitted.
Judges★	Theater professionals.
Winner Notification★	Notification of preliminary selections is made in the spring. Final selections take place in early summer.
Awards★	Production of the play in the Young Playwrights Festival in New York City. Authors participate in casting and rehearsal of their plays. Playwrights also receive transportation, housing, royalties, and complimentary 1-year membership in the Dramatists Guild.

Competition★	**Youth for Understanding International Exchange**
Sponsor★	Youth for Understanding USA 6400 Goldsboro Road Ste. 100 Bethesda, MD 20817
Web Address★	http://www.yfu-usa.org
Area★	Academic recognition
Competition Origin★	1952
Purpose★	To provide scholarships for students to participate in international exchanges.
Description★	Youth for Understanding International Exchange administers full or partial scholarship programs for American students to study overseas. Guidelines may be obtained on the Web site or by writing to the sponsor.
Eligibility★	Students ages 15–18.
Important Dates★	Scholarship applications are due in January and early spring. See guidelines for specific dates.
How to Enter★	Students must complete an application form and be nominated by a principal, teacher, or guidance counselor.
Judging Criteria★	For most year and semester programs, a B average or better (3.0 on a 4.0 scale) is required. For summer programs, a C average or better (2.0 on a 4.0 scale) is required; however, a 3.0 GPA or higher may be required in some cases
Judges★	Corporate sponsors for each scholarship.
Winner Notification★	Winners are notified prior to the start of program.
Awards★	Scholarships include:

- professional orientation programs and materials;
- all group international air travel costs and assistance from YFU travel staff at international gateway airports;
- domestic air travel costs from a YFU-designated airport;
- local and regional trips and educational activities while you're overseas (where noted);
- placement with a carefully screened YFU host family;

- support through counseling, tutoring, and other means;
- training for volunteers who provide professional, individual support for you and your host family;
- 24-hour worldwide professional emergency assistance;
- enrollment in school if your scholarship is for a year or semester program;
- assistance in acquiring your visa or residence permit if required;
- the 1-800-TEENAGE line staffed with friendly and knowledgeable Admissions Counselors to answer all of your questions.

Advice★

Many scholarships are designated for a specific country. Others allow you to list several country choices. You should think carefully about which countries interest you most.

★ PART II ★
Competitions Journal

★ ★

Why I Want to Enter a Competition

Think of the many great reasons you want to enter competitions. List them and keep them in mind throughout your preparation and participation in competitions.

- _____
- _____
- _____
- _____
- _____
- _____
- _____
- _____
- _____
- _____
- _____
- _____
- _____
- _____
- _____
- _____

★ ★

Top 10 Competitions I'd Like to Enter

What competitions interest you? In which competitions can you see yourself as a terrific participant? Choose your top 10 competitions and list them in rank order from your most favorite to your least favorite. As you begin competing you can change your list.

1. _____

2. _____

3. _____

4. _____

5. _____

6. _____

7. _____

8. _____

9. _____

10. _____

Letter to Obtain Competition Information

From time to time you may hear of additional competitions or need more information on a specific one. A short letter requesting the details will usually get a quick reply. Be sure to include a self-addressed, stamped envelope with your letter. Some competitions may not reply to your letter if this is not included. This sample letter will serve as a guide for you.

Date

Your Name
Street Address
City, State Zip Code

Competition Name
Street Address
City, State Zip Code

Dear (insert name of contact if known; otherwise use Sir or Madam),

The (insert name of competition) competition is of interest to me and I would like to request more information. Please send me any materials you might have on the purpose, requirements, and awards. I have included a self-addressed, stamped envelope for your convenience.

Thank you for responding to this request.

Sincerely,

Your name

My Competition Goals

What are your competition goals? In which competitions would you like to be involved? What skills would you like to sharpen? With whom would you like to meet and share your ideas? Competitions can lead to the accomplishment of many personal goals. Find a nice quiet place to sit and think about your goals and how you plan to achieve them through competitions. Write down your thoughts. As you meet your goals, decide on new ones.

GOAL:

STEPS TO ACHIEVING MY GOAL:

1.

2.

3.

4.

5.

GOAL:

STEPS TO ACHIEVING MY GOAL:

1.

2.

3.

4.

5.

The Spirit of Competition!

Think about the spirit of competition . . . specifically yours! How do you feel or think you will feel before, during, and after a competition? Write down the ways you feel and the causes of those feelings.

Before a competition, I may feel or have felt . . .

During a competition, I may feel or have felt . . .

After a competition, I may feel or have felt . . .

Things I can do to make myself feel better . . .

★ ★

How I Selected a Competition

Reflect upon the process you went through in order to select a competition in which you want to participate or have done so. List the many reasons for your selection. You may want to add to this list with each new competition you enter.

My Talents and Abilities:

My Interests:

My Resources:

The Guidelines:

Awards:

Other:

★ ★

Time Management Tips

As you begin planning for and participating in competitions, you'll quickly find the importance and value of managing your time well. You can do it by following these tips. As you learn to manage your time, write down what works for you—your very own time management tips.

- *Set priorities.* Decide what is the most important task and do it first. It may help to write down your goals in order of importance.

- *Be flexible.* Remember, sometimes things change. Take advantage of opportunities to try something different.

- *Plan time to get organized.* Just getting organized takes a few minutes. Grab your calendar, list of goals, and competition information; find a comfortable place to sit; and start organizing and planning.

- *Use little bits of time.* There are times you can use to complete small jobs, like waiting on the bus, TV commercial breaks during your favorite show, or in between classes. Find something small and get it done.

- *Set deadlines.* Decide when you'd like to have your goals met. Be sure to check off each one as you complete it. If you finish before a deadline, good for you!

- *Make and use lists.* Write down your plans for getting ready for the competition. As you finish each step, celebrate by marking it off.

- *Use calendars or appointment books.* These are great tools for staying on top of things. A sample calendar is provided in this book. Use it or one of your own.

- *My Time Management Tips.*

  - •   •

  - •   •

  - •   •

My Competition Calendar

Keeping important dates straight is one of the keys to success in competition. Depending upon your individual style and preference, a calendar of some sort will help you do just that. There are many different types of calendars: pocket, wall, weekly, and monthly, to name a few. Perhaps you have a computer program with a calendar. Select the one that's best for you.

Here's a sample:

DAY OF WEEK	THINGS TO DO TODAY
SUNDAY	
MONDAY	
TUESDAY	
WEDNESDAY	
THURSDAY	
FRIDAY	
SATURDAY	

Things I Need for the Competition

As you prepare for a competition, think about the items you will need for success. List the items you will need, marking those you have and those you will need to acquire. Determine where you will get those items you don't yet have.

Items required:	I have these:	I'll have to get these from:
•	•	•
•	•	•
•	•	•
•	•	•
•	•	•
•	•	•
•	•	•
•	•	•
•	•	•
•	•	•
•	•	•

Phone Calls

The telephone can be a great tool for asking questions and finding answers, networking with others, and sharing good news. It's important to use good phone manners. Plan your conversation and be certain to write down any important information you receive. This phone form may help you.

"Hello, my name is (your name). May I please speak to (name of person) or someone who can give me information about the (name of competition)?"

"I am calling (state the reason you are calling). . . ." (You should prepare what you are going to say ahead of time. Use the space below to write down your thoughts.)

What information did you receive? Write down what you are told by your contact.

"Thank you very much. I appreciate your help." After you have received the needed information, be sure to conclude the call by letting the person know that you appreciate his or her time and help.

Be sure to write the date and time of the call, as well as the name and phone number of the person with whom you spoke.

Date and Time:

Contact Person's Name:

Contact Person's Phone Number:

Sponsor, Sponsor . . . Who's Got a Sponsor?

Competitions sometimes require a school or community sponsor. Other times, sponsors can be located to give support in terms of advice, money, and/or time and goods/services. But how do you get a sponsor? It's easy. Just follow these steps!

- Gather all the facts and details about the competition in which you are interested. Read about it. Be sure you clearly understand the competition.

- Write down exactly why you need a sponsor and what you need the sponsor to do. Think about what you will say when you speak to the potential sponsor. You might even want to practice the conversation with someone else.

- Brainstorm individuals or businesses in your school and community who may be willing and able to help you. You may want to ask your parents, teachers, or friends to assist you as you put together this list.

- You may want to look in the yellow pages of your telephone directory or call the local Chamber of Commerce for possible sponsors.

- Contact the sponsor by phone or a letter. Ask if you can set up an appointment or special time to meet so that you can discuss your competition plans and ideas.

- Go visit your sponsor. Be sure you are on time and look nice. Manners are important, too, so use only the best. Notes and information about the competition may be helpful, so take them. You might want to have an extra copy to leave with the possible sponsor. Smile!

- Be sure to thank your sponsor after the contest is over. A little thanks goes a long way. Remember to let them know how much you enjoyed being a part of the contest in which you entered. Write a thank you note with details of the competition you were able to enter with their help.

★ ★

Great Lessons I've Learned

Competitions can teach us a lot of things about our interests, our strengths, our abilities, and ourselves. We can learn more about our work habits, attitudes, and goals for the future as we meet others, plan projects, and have fun. Think about the great lessons you will or have learned about competitions.

**Through competition
I will learn:**

**Through competition I have
learned more about:**

My interests

My interests

My strengths

My strengths

My abilities

My abilities

My attitudes

My attitudes

My work habits

My work habits

My goals

My goals

My List of Recognitions

There are many different kinds of recognition given for participation in competitions. You may receive a medal, trophy, certificate, money, or even a trip. What types of recognition would you like to receive? Better yet, how have you already been recognized?

List of Recognitions
I Would Like to Receive

-
-
-
-
-

List of Recognitions I Have
Already Received

-
-
-
-
-

My Slogan for Competitions

What are your feelings and attitudes about competitions? Sum it all up in a slogan. Write a catchy, creative slogan for competitions. Share your ideas with others through a poster, T-shirt design, bumper sticker, play—the possibilities are endless.

Competitions Are Fun

Planning and participating in competitions will involve work, but also you'll have tons of fun. You will use your mind in new ways, learn to develop a variety of products, meet new friends, develop and enhance your personal and social skills, and perhaps travel to new and different places. Keeping these memories of all the fun activities will be great. Perhaps you'll want to share these exciting experiences with your friends through discussions, letters, e-mail, editorials in your school or local newspaper, a TV or radio interview, or a dozen other ways.

WAYS I'VE HAD FUN THROUGH COMPETITIONS

- _____

- _____

- _____

- _____

- _____

- _____

- _____

- _____

- _____

- _____

- _____

- _____

* *

Being Recognized

Being in competitions may bring recognition to you, your school, and your community. A great way to share your accomplishments is through a press release to be sent to newspapers, television, and/or radio. Look in your local telephone book for the addresses. You may use the format below to notify others of your accomplishments.

PRESS RELEASE

(Your name) participated in the (competition name) on (date) in (city, state). (He/She) is a (your grade) grade student at (your school) in (city, state). The (competition name) is designed to (purpose of competition). (Add more detailed information as you see fit.)

Thank You Letter

Thank you letters are a great way to show your appreciation to the many people who have been encouraging and supportive of you entering a competition. You may want to write to your teacher, sponsor, parents, friends, and others. Don't forget to say kind words to the people who were responsible for running the competition. They have worked hard to make it a great event.

Here is a sample thank you note. You'll want to use your own special way of expressing your appreciation.

Date

Your Name
Street Address
City, State Zip Code

Competition or Contact's Name
Street Address
City, State Zip Code

Dear (insert name of contact if known; otherwise use Sir or Madam),

Thank you for the opportunity to participate in (name of competition). I learned (mention what you have learned from participating in this competition). You were very helpful, and I appreciate (cite something specific that you appreciate). (Add more information as needed.)

Sincerely,

Your name

What Else Is Out There?

There are many opportunities available for you to share your talents and abilities through competitions. We've given you quite a few national ones from which to chose, but there may be others you'd like to try. As you discover local, regional, state, and national contests of interest, record the information. Share these other contests with your friends.

Competition:

Contact Person:

Address:

Area of Competition:

Date:

Competition:

Contact Person:

Address:

Area of Competition:

Date:

*Your computer can be a useful tool to help you keep up with this information. Create a database of competitions.

Start a Competition Club

Wouldn't it be fun to share your successes and good ideas with your friends? Why not start a competition club? You and your fellow members can share information about upcoming contests, discuss the ups and downs of competing, and best of all, form a network of friends. Before starting your club, think about the following questions.

What will be the purpose of your club?

Who will be able to join your club?

How will new members join?

When and where will your club meet?

Who will help you get your club started?

How will you let others know about your club?

How will you obtain permission to start a club, if indeed permission is needed?

How will you keep the club going?

Will you charge a membership fee?

★ ★

Let's Hear From You!

You are important to us and we would like to hear from you with your ideas and comments about this book and your participation in competitions. We encourage you to write to us.

I am a:
- ❐ student
- ❐ teacher
- ❐ guidance counselor
- ❐ school administrator
- ❐ competition director
- ❐ other

1. What is your favorite competition(s) and why?

2. What have you learned by participating in competition(s)?

3. If you have participated in national competitions other than the ones listed in this book, please share the information.

_____

Name of Competition

_____

Address

_____

City, State, Zip

4. What suggestions do you have for additional information for this book?

5. Other comments

****

Mail this form to:
Dr. Frances A. Karnes
University of Southern Mississippi
Box 8207
Hattiesburg, MS 39406-8207

★ PART III ★
Resources

Photography

Alesse, C. (2000). *Basic 35MM photo guide: For beginning photographers*. Buffalo, NY: Amherst Media.

Ancona, G. (1992). *My camera*. New York: Crown Books for Young Readers.

Bown, D. (1995). *101 essential tips: Photography*. New York: DK Publishing.

Burian, P., & Caputo, R. (2003). *National Geographic photography field guide: Secrets to making great pictures*. Washington, DC: National Geographic Society.

Evans, A. (1993). *First photos: How kids can take great pictures*. Redondo Beach, CA: Photo Data Resources.

Ewald, W., & Lightfoot, A. (2002). *I wanna take me a picture: Teaching photography and writing to children*. New York: Beacon Press.

Friedman, D., & Kurisu, J. (2003). *Picture this: Fun photography and crafts*. Toronto, ON: Kids CanPress, Limited.

Gibbons, G. (1997). *Click!: A book about cameras and taking pictures*. New York: Little, Brown & Company.

Gleason, R. (1992). *Seeing yourself: Techniques and projects for beginning photographers*. Chicago: Chicago Review.

Grimm, T., & Grimm, M. (1998). *Basic book of photography*. Dumont, NJ: Penguin USA.

Hedgecoe, J. (2003). *The new manual of photography: The definitive guide to photography*. New York: DK Publishing.

Hilton, J., & Watts, B. (1994). *Photography*. Brookfield, CT: The Millbrook Press.

Jeunesse, G. (1993). *The camera: Snapshots, movies, videos, and cartoons*. New York: Scholastic.

Jimison, C. (2001). *Tricky pix: Do-it-yourself trick photography with camera*. Palo Alto, CA: Klutz.

Johnson, N. (2001). *National Geographic photography guide for kids*. Washington, DC: National Geographic Society.

Kodak Company. (1995). *Kodak pocket guide to 35mm photography*. Hauppauge, NY: Silver Pixel Press.

Langford, M. (1993). *Starting photography*. Stoneham, MA: Focal Press.

Limpus, B. (1994). *Lights! Camera! Action!: A guide to using video production in the classroom*. Waco, TX: Prufrock Press.

Marsh, C. (1994). *Hot shot: Photography for kids*. Atlanta, GA: Gallapad Publishing Group.

Morgan, T. & Thaler, S. (1991). *Photography: Take your best shot.* Minneapolis, MN: Lerner Publishing.

Oxlade, C. (2000). *Cameras.* Hawthorne, NJ: Anness Publishing, Ltd.

Wilson, K. (1994). *Photography.* New York: Knopf Books for Young Readers.

Speeches

Barlow, B. (2002). *Oral presentations made easy: Super strategies and warm-ups that help kids write and give effective speeches and presentations—and communication with confidence.* New York: Scholastic.

Carratello, P. (1981). *I can give a speech.* Westminster, CA: Teacher Created Materials.

Cocetti, R. A., & Snyder, L. (1992). *Talk that matters: An introduction to public speaking.* Kearney, NE: Education Systems Association.

Colligan, L. (1989). *A-Plus junior guide to giving a speech.* New York: Scholastic.

Detz, J. (1986). *You mean I have to stand up and say something?* New York: Macmillan Children's Group.

Dunbar, R. E. (1990). *Making your point.* New York: Watts.

Gower, S. M. (1998). *Missing lynx: Finally, a speak-in-public learning system for high school students.* Marin County, CA: Lectern Publishing.

Kramme, M. (1996). *How to prepare and give a speech.* Quincy, IL: Mark Twain Media.

McCutcheon, R. (1993). *Communication matters.* Saint Paul, MN: West Publication.

Murphy, T. J., & Snyder, K. (1995). *What! I have to give a speech?* Bloomington, IN: Grayson Bernard Publishing.

Otfinoski, S. (1996). *Speaking up, speaking out: A student's guide to public speaking.* Southampton, NY: Millbrook Press.

Ryan, M. (1996). *How to give a speech.* Woods Cross, UT: Scholastic Library.

Visual Arts

Arnold, T. (1996). *My first drawing book.* New York: Workman Publication.

Auvil, K. (1998). *Perspective drawing.* Houston, TX: Mayfield Publishing.

Barish, W. (1983). *I can draw horses.* New York: S&S Trade.

Barry, J. (1990). *Draw, design, and paint.* Carthage, IL: Good Apple.

Baxter, L. (1993). *The drawing book.* Nashville, TN: Hambleton-Hill.

Biddle, M., & Biddle, S. (1994). *Origami safari.* New York: Tupelo Books.

Borgeson, B. (1995). *The colored pencil: Key concepts for handling the medium.* New York: BPI Communications.

Bradley, S. (1992). *How to draw cartoons.* Aspen, CO: Mad Hatter.

Bullock, P., & North, P. (2000). *Charcoal pocket studio.* New York: Watson-Guptill Publications.

Butterfield, M. (1988). *How to draw machines.* Tulsa, OK: EDC.

Connor, N. (1996). *Creative crafts from cardboard boxes.* Brookfield, CT: Copper Beach Books.

Connor, N. (1996). *Creative crafts from plastic cups.* Brookfield, CT: Copper Beach Books.

Connor, N. (1997). *Creative crafts from cardboard tubes.* Brookfield, CT: Copper Beach Books.

Connor, N. (1997). *Creative crafts from plastic bottles.* Brookfield, CT: Copper Beach Books.

Craig, D. (1993). *Making models.* Brookfield, CT: The Millbrook Press.

David, M. (1993). *Cartooning for kids: A step-by-step guide to creating your own cartoons.* New York: Harper Collins.

DK Publishing Staff. (2003). *My animals art class.* New York: DK Publishing.

DK Publishing Staff. (2003). *My art class: Kitchen crafts.* New York: DK Publishing.

Dr. Seuss. (1987). *I can draw it myself: By me, myself with a little help from my friend Dr. Seuss.* New York: Beginner.

DuBosque, D. (1998). *Draw 3-D.* Columbus, NC: Peel Productions.

Everett, F. (1987). *Usborne guide to fashion design.* London: Usborne Publishing Ltd.

Fleischman, P. (1993). *Copier creations: Using copy machines to make decals, silhouettes, flip books, films, and much more!* New York: Harper Collins Children's Books.

Foster, W. (1998). *Fun with printing.* Laguna Hills, CA: Walter Foster Publishing.

Freeberg, E., & Freeberg D. (1987). *Simple graph art.* Westminster, CA: Teacher Created Material.

Gair, A. (1997). *How to draw and paint people.* Laguna Hills, CA: Walter Foster Publishing.

Gamble, K. (1994). *You can draw anything.* Australia: A Little Ark Book.

Gibson, R. (1993). *The Usborne book of masks.* London: Usborne Publishing Ltd.

Gibson, R. (1995). *The Usborne book of paper mache.* London: Usborne Publishing Ltd.

Gibson, R. (1996). *The Usborne book of printing.* London: Usborne Publishing Ltd.

Hart, C. (2003). *Kids draw animals.* New York: Watson-Guptill Publications.

Heller, R. (1992). *Designs for coloring optical art.* New York: Putnam Publication Group.

Irvine, J. (1991). *How to make pop-ups.* New York: Beach Tree Paperback Book.

Kistler, M. (2003). *Dare to draw in 3-D: Cartoon critters.* New York: Scholastic.

Lade, R. (1996). *The most excellent book of how to be a puppeteer.* Brookfield, CT: Copper Beach Books.

Lightfoot, M. (1993). *Cartooning for kids.* Buffalo, NY: Firefly Books Limited.

Martin, J. (1993). *Painting and drawing.* Brookfield, CT: The Millbrook Press.

Milbourne, A. (2003). *Drawing cartoons.* Tulsa, OK: Usborne Publishing.

Novak, J.T. (1996). *You can make mobiles.* Australia: A Little Ark Book.

O'Connor, J. (2002). *Henri Matisse: Drawing with scissors.* New York: Grosset & Dunlap.

Potter, T. (1987). *The Usborne book of graphic design.* London: Usborne Publishing Ltd.

Rakel-Ferguson, K. (2002). *Creative kids artistic drawing.* Cincinnati, OH: F & W Publications.

Reece, N. (2002). *The Usborne complete book of drawing.* Tulsa, OK: Usborne Publishing.

Simblet, S. (2001). *Anatomy for the artist.* New York: DK Publishing.

Sirett, D. (1994). *My first paint book.* New York: DK Publishing.

Tatchell, J., & Evans, C. (1987). *Young cartoonist.* Tulsa, OK: EDC.

Tollison, H. (1989). *Cartoon fun.* Tustin, CA: W Foster Publication.

Vaughan, G., & Jackson (1990). *Sketching and drawing for children.* New York: Putnam Publication Group.

Wright, M. (1998). *An introduction to pastels.* New York: DK Publishing.

Writing

Arnsteen, K., Bentley, N., & Guthrie, D. (1994). *The young author's do-it-yourself book*. Brookfield, CT: The Millbrook Press.

Artman, J. H. (1985). *The write stuff!* Carthage, IL: Good Apple.

Bauer, M.D. (1992). *What's your story? A young person's guide to writing fiction*. Boston: Houghton Mifflin.

Bentley, N., & Guthrie, D. (1996). *Putting on a play: The young playwright's guide to scripting, directing, and performing*. Brookfield, CT: The Millbrook Press.

Broekel, R. (1986). *I can be an author*. Chicago: Childrens.

Buhay, D. (1990). *Black and white of writing*. Allentown, PA: Hockenberry.

Cassedy, S. (1990). *In your own words: A beginner's guide to writing*. New York: Harper Collins Children's Books.

Chapman, G., & Robson, P. (1991). *Making books: A step-by-step to your own publishing*. Brookfield, CT: The Millbrook Press.

Chapman, G., & Robson, P. (1993). *Making shaped books*. Brookfield, CT: The Millbrook Press.

Daniel, B. (1990). *Writing brainstorms*. Carthage, IL: Good Apple.

Dunn, D., & Dunn J. (1996). *Teen's guide to getting published*. Waco, TX: Prufrock Press.

Fleisher, P. (1989). *Write now*. Carthage, IL: Good Apple.

Fletcher, R. J. (1996). *A writer's notebook: Unlocking the writer within you*. New York: Avon Books.

Fletcher, R. J. (2000). *How writers work: Finding a process that works for you*. New York: Harper Collins.

Fletcher, R. J. (1999). *Live writing: Breathing life into your words*. New York: Avon Books.

Fletcher, R. J. (2002). *Poetry matters: Writing a poem from the inside out*. New York: Harper Collins.

Fletcher, R. J. (1992). *What a writer needs*. New York: Reed Elsevier Incorporated.

James, E. (1998). *How to write terrific book reports*. New York: William Morrow & Company.

Kellaher, K. (2001). *Writing skills made fun: Parts of speech*. New York: Scholastic.

Mammen, L. (1989). *Writing warm-ups*. San Antonio, TX: ECS Learning Systems.

Polette, N. (1997). *Research reports to knock your teacher's socks off!* Marion, IL: Pieces of Learning

Ryan, E. (1992). *How to be a better writer.* Bronxville, NY: Troll Association.

Ryan, E. (1992). *How to write better book reports.* Bronxville, NY: Troll Association.

Stanish, B. (1983). *Creativity for kids through writing.* Carthage, IL: Good Apple.

Tchudi, S., & Tchudi, S. (1987). *The young writer's handbook: A practical guide for the beginner who is serious about writing.* New York: Macmillan Children's Group.

Whitfield, J. (1994). *Getting kids published: A practical guide for helping young authors see their works in print.* Waco, TX: Prufrock Press.